WHAT HAPPENED NEXT?

GEORGE W. HOYER

WHAT HAPPENED NEXT?

Nine Messages on Some of Jesus' Great Acts and Stories

AUGSBURG Publishing House • Minneapolis

WHAT HAPPENED NEXT?
Nine Messages on Some of Jesus' Great Acts and Stories

Copyright © 1987 Augsburg Publishing House

All rights reserved. Except for brief quotations in critical articles or reviews, no part of this book may be reproduced in any manner without prior written permission from the publisher. Write to: Permissions, Augsburg Publishing House, 426 S. Fifth St., Box 1209, Minneapolis MN 55440.

Scripture quotations unless otherwise noted are from the Revised Standard Version of the Bible, copyright 1946, 1952, and 1971 by the Division of Christian Education of the National Council of Churches.

Library of Congress Cataloging-in-Publication Data

Hoyer, George W.
 What happened next?

 1. Lenten sermons. 2. Sermons, American.
3. Lutheran Church—Sermons. I. Title.
BV4277.H63   1987   252'.62   87-30814
ISBN 0-8066-2299-7

Manufactured in the U.S.A.   APH 10-7049

 1 2 3 4 5 6 7 8 9 0 1 2 3 4 5 6 7 8 9

CONTENTS

Preface 9

Thomas, Richard—and Me
Luke 15:11-32 13

This Little Child Says Yes
Matthew 21:28-32 23

Getting Back into the Vineyard After the Payoff of Grace
Matthew 20:1-16 35

Let's Do It Again
Mark 2:1-12 45

The Daughter of Jairus Raised Again
Mark 5:21-24, 35-43 55

Next Best to Jesus
*Matthew 26:26-28; Mark 14:22-24; Luke 22:14-20;
1 Corinthians 11:23-25* 65

70 x 7 —490 and Counting
Matthew 18:21-35 77

Easter without Spices
Mark 16:1-8 87

He Goes with You
Matthew 16:13-25 99

PREFACE

These are sermons suggested for use from Ash Wednesday to Easter. Pastors might find here suggestions for narrative sermons in a topical series. The series can follow the sequence of the sermons as ordered in the contents. Their accents can mesh with the Wednesdays in Lent, including a witnessing message for the Wednesday of Easter week, or with Sunday evenings through Easter Sunday. In story form they deal with important Christian teachings. Based on biblical texts, they ask, "What if . . . ?" and reach out beyond the text. "Helps for Hearers" are given for possible use in a discussion forum preceding the service and the sermon. Hearers could thus be helped in advance to make their own applications as the stories unfold. The impact of the narratives and the unity of the worship would then not be dulled by a late insertion of explanation.

These sermons need not be limited to the pulpit and preachers. Those who usually only listen to sermons can be helped here by reading and meditating. They can use the "Helps" to check their own interpretations of the messages.

❦

In the beginning of time, the Word was with God, and was God—and was creative.

Somewhere in the middle of time (as it seems to us, at least) the Word was with people in Palestine and was made God-in-Christ—and was redeeming.

These are the last days, the end of time. (They are called the last days in Scripture, and to many, they seem to last and last.) The Word works still, creating, redeeming. God-in-Christ is with us always to the end of the age, and the Spirit of God now blows where the Spirit wills—sanctifying.

The Word is available to remembrance and reflection. The Word's power is released in splashing and eating and drinking, in the interaction of believers, in reading and in sermons.

Is not the Word also available in imagination? The Lord entered the lives of sick and well, rich and poor, friends and enemies, in those years he was visible. But from each group he went on to others. The impact of his presence, the memories of his words and deeds, did not go away. People carried him along in mind all the way to death, and beyond, to life again. People remembered, people wished: "Oh, if only he had been here!" People imagined: "Will you at this time . . . ?" "When you come into your kingdom . . ." And the Word worked on, in recollection and anticipation—and in imagination.

These sermons recollect what the Word did, dwelling among us, what the Word did, telling stories among us. To that they add—imagination: "What if . . . ?" They work to have the Word keep on doing what the Word did.

"God chose . . . even things that are not. . . ." (1 Cor. 1:28).

Preface

Christ Seminary–Seminex and Pacific Lutheran Theological Seminary made study leaves for this writing available, and grants from Lutheran Brotherhood and Aid Association for Lutherans helped to make them possible. Thanks are due to all their membership and to all who support the seminaries.

conversion
repentance

THOMAS, RICHARD—AND ME

The Prodigal and Justification by Grace

Luke 15:11-32

Helps for Hearing

The prodigal "came to himself," which implies that he had somehow "left himself."

Imagine a conversation between husband Adam and wife Eve the morning after they had eaten of the forbidden fruit:

"What's the matter?"

"What do you mean, 'What's the matter?'"

"You're not yourself today."

Surely that is fact. To sin is to stop being the self we have been made to be. It is as if God had said, "In the day you disobey you shall surely stop being your self." It's true about us all. When we sin, the image of God in which we were created is distorted and blurred. The self that could stand before God in righteousness and true holiness disappears and hides in the bushes. The self able to resist evil and choose good now does the evil it really doesn't want to do and doesn't do the good it wishes it would.

What must be done if we are to "come to our self" again?

The son whom we call the *prodigal* was certainly not himself. Sitting on the fence by the pigsty, wishing he could still his hunger by eating what the pigs ate, he was almost beside himself. So full of regret, forsaken by all his friends—certainly he was *by* himself. But was it possible for him to *come to* himself *by* himself?

The answer is important to us. All we like prodigals have gone astray—and that not only once, for one fling in a far country, but repeatedly. Time after time we leave home and leave our Father and leave our true self. Can we come to our true self by our self?

The father in the story does not say, "At last you've come to yourself." He has it right: "He was lost, and is found." Scripture agrees: we cannot come to ourselves but by the Holy Spirit. Someone must come to seek and to save the lost. God, taking on "self" in Jesus Christ came to bring us to ourselves. The church calls what God did once for all, "justification by grace." Believe it. It is received by faith. What happened to us by that grace is called *conversion*. We are turned around, turned back to the right direction.

That kind of conversion, Jesus said, is like being born again. Most of us experienced that new birth with little personal awareness at our baptisms. Some of us, however, were very aware of that conversion, when first by the gift of faith we grasped that God in Christ had made us members of God's family.

Think now about the many, the repeated, "conversions" that take place in our lives. Whenever in anger or frustration we storm out of the family living room and slam our bedroom door behind us, some sort of "conversion" must take place if we are to return to the family circle. We call that returning *repentance*. We must "come to our self" as the prodigal did, before we rejoin father and mother and sister and brother. How does it happen, this "coming to our self"? What is it that brings us back to our selves? It is vital that we know, because we need that power so many times. It is important that we know, for if we know where that power comes from, we can turn to the true source for true selfness.

Probably we are all more like the older brother than the prodigal. The older brother resented his younger brother. He was angry, he was envious, he refused to have anything to do with him. Jesus told this story originally to shake up those critics who complained about how he gave loving attention to "sinners," to those his enemies regarded as "unconverted," as "unrepentant." The point of the story for those enemies was how much the older brother needed to "come to himself," to repent.

The "rest of the story" then is about us all, really, all of us who repeatedly need to come to our selves. What is it that restores in us the love for brother, sister, father, that increases in us the love for the father's house? If we know how it happens, can we not help in its happening?

That is what we will meditate on. In the story that follows, we will focus on how the prodigal was brought to himself, on how the older brother, on how all of us, over and over again, are found and are brought to ourselves.

The Rest of the Story

Most of you know my father, at least. I've met most of you before. You may not recognize me, not by name anyway. Perhaps you'll remember who I am as I tell you about what happened at our house, what happened to my father and my two brothers.

You know my brother Tom. He's the oldest, a bit stodgy, perhaps, but steady. Does his work, does everything that's expected of him. Not much of a sense of humor, not much fun, not like Dick.

WHAT HAPPENED NEXT?

Dick is my other brother. You know him better, perhaps. You call him *the prodigal,* because, as all of you know who have heard his story, "he squandered his property in loose living" (Luke 15:13). Well, he did. No doubt of that.

He collected his inheritance early. Father was reluctant and full of concern. "Of course you should grow up and be on your own," he said to Dick. "Of course you have to choose what you're going to do and not do ... of course you must take responsibility," he said. But what hurt father was that really Dick wanted to get out of the family, away from home—out from under father. But father finally conceded, hoping against his fears.

And so Dick went off on his own to a far country. It seemed far away to him then, but it really was not much farther than the far edge of this state. And, it's true, he did squander it all in loose living.

It was my older brother, Tom, who complained bitterly about Dick to father. "He's squandered your livelihood with prostitutes." He was angry then, and he stayed angry. He stayed home and didn't leave father, but I'm not sure that said much about what he actually felt.

For Dick there was no excuse. He did make a fool of himself. But still I missed him. I really loved him. Father did too—loved him and missed him. And so I urged father to let me go find him and try to persuade him to come home. We had heard that he had run through everything he had and had hired himself out—of all things—to a farmer who set him to tending hogs.

"Let me go to him," I said to father, "and let him know how much we miss him, how much we love him." Of course, he should have known that—but just considering all the fool things he had done, I suspected he really wasn't himself. I thought if I could just get him to remember—really remember—what it's like here at home, maybe he'd come to himself and change and come home.

Thomas, Richard—and Me

Father wasn't so sure. After all, he had argued and reasoned with Dick long enough before he left. And he probably knew it wouldn't be easy—Dick's so-called "friends" would give me a rough time. But finally Father agreed—even asked me to go, urged me to go. And so I set about preparing.

(And now you must let your imaginations run a bit, because, of course, it couldn't have been quite like this. But imagine it.)

I went down to the kitchen where the cook was just pulling some fresh-baked bread out of the oven. You know how wonderful it is in the kitchen then! How glorious the bread smells and how it fills all the house with a homey feeling, its crust brown and flaky, and inside so risen up, so soft and warm and so—well, *bread!* I asked the cook for a loaf of that bread and carefully wrapped it in aluminum foil to keep it fresh and bundled it up with the morning newspaper to keep it warm. I put the bread in a picnic basket and went out to the well house, where every morning the wine for the day is always placed so that it will be cool. I selected a bottle of the Grey Riesling, which Dick always liked, and wrapped it carefully, too, so that the bottle wouldn't break, and it would stay cool as if just from the well. I put the wine into the basket, too.

And off I went.

I found him, but I had a hard time of it. Those old friends of Dick were certainly not his friends any longer, and I won't tell you the kind of abuse and ridicule and even anger and hatred I put up with. According to them, there was evidently something very wrong in our family that had made Dick leave home. They blamed father for expecting too much, for making unreasonable demands on Dick. Somehow it was all father's fault that the money had run out and that Dick was broke. And I got it too—somehow if I had managed things better, Dick wouldn't have done what he did, and things wouldn't have turned out the way they

WHAT HAPPENED NEXT?

had, and Dick wouldn't have become what he'd become—a swineherd.

There he was, sitting on the wooden fence at the edge of the field where the farmer's hogs were rooting, and he looked almost hungry enough to snatch some of the bean pods the pigs were eating.

I walked up behind him and, of course, I spoke his name: "Dick."

He turned and saw me, and suddenly his face turned all white and then blushed red and embarrassed, and he turned away. You could tell he knew how foolishly he had acted, but there was an immediate defense and a sort of defiance in his voice, and he said, "Let me alone. It's my own business what I do. I'm my own man, and I can do what I like. Anyway, who cares?"

Who cares? That he could think that! It wasn't the Dick I knew. He really wasn't himself.

I knew then what I had to do—to make sure he knew we loved him. I just started to talk of how it was at home, about our rooms, and the things we had collected on our shelves and how fresh the fields were in the morning, and father's voice day after day waking us with that dreadfully cheery, "Rise and shine!" or singing, "The Morning Bright." He smiled a bit then; we used to hate that song so! But I'm sure that remembering it was remembering how much father loved us.

Then I did some other "remember" things. "Remember how, after father had specially told us not to, we went to play in the old pasture over the hill way beyond the barn? Remember that old abandoned well there?"

(I don't know if you know about Palestinian wells. They must dig them down deep in order to find water, and then if the well runs dry, they abandon them. They cover them over but it doesn't take long to forget where the old wells are. Then the rain and sun make the covers rotten and treacherous. That's why father was so serious when he

Thomas, Richard—and Me

warned us about them. "In the day you go down to that old field to play you shall surely die." But of course we did. Dick practically said, "Let's do it because we shouldn't." And we did.)

I reminded Dick how we suddenly decided we wanted to look down the well and see how deep it was, and just as we were dragging the last board away, the edge crumbled and he fell in all the way into the muck and spiders at the bottom. Just thinking about it again had me almost crying and I said to Dick, "All I could do was to cry out, 'I'm going for father!' and hope you could hear me at the bottom of the well. I ran to find him and I told him what we had done and what had happened. He only cried out, 'Oh, Dick!' and said not a word more. He dropped everything he was doing and started running. When we got to the well, he crawled on his stomach right to the edge of the well and looked down. Remember, Dick, how glad you said you were when that little circle of light at the top of the well, which was all that you could see, was broken and you knew it was father's face up against the sky? And all he said was, 'O Richard! My son, my son!'

"Then father turned to me and said, 'Run and get the servants and tell them to bring two coils of rope from the barn.' And meanwhile—remember Dick?—father didn't just stand there looking around. He clambered down—'to be with Dick,' that's what he explained later. There were a few footholds and handholds at first to support him, but then he slipped and fell the last distance and landed with a crash right next to you."

Then Dick interrupted me. "What I remember most—he didn't say anything, didn't bawl me out. He just hugged me. He just sat with me and hugged me."

"Well . . . the servants came and let the ropes down and pulled. And how wonderful it was to see your head and then your shoulders and arms coming up out of the well, like rising from a grave. And then father. And even then he didn't

WHAT HAPPENED NEXT?

say anything like, 'How could you?' or like that. He just wiped your face, which—admit it—was stained with tears, and he tousled your hair. It was just as if he'd said, 'It's O.K. Your sin is forgiven.'"

I expected Dick to be as happy as I in remembering, but I looked directly at him and saw he looked as downcast as if he had lost all hope, and he said, "And now I've done it again. And this is worse."

I didn't say any more. I just took the bread and carefully unwrapped it. It was still warm and crispy and smelled so good and he knew it was from home. I broke off a piece for him and a piece for me. Then I unwrapped the wine, and he saw it was the Riesling. I poured some for him and for me. And then I said very quietly, "Morning after morning father walks to the gate and looks down the road as if waiting, waiting for you to come home."

And that's how he came to himself.
Now, have you guessed who I am?
You know Tom. You know Dick.
You think I'm Harry?
No. You're Harry—or Harriet.
I'm their sister.
My name is Mercy.

❦

>Today your mercy calls us
>To wash away our sin.
>However great our trespass,
>Whatever we have been,
>However long from mercy
>Our hearts have turned away,
>Your precious blood can wash us
>And make us clean today.
>
>Today your gate is open,
>And all who enter in

Thomas, Richard—and Me

Shall find a Father's welcome
And pardon for their sin.
The past shall be forgotten,
A present joy be giv'n,
A future grace be promised,
A glorious crown in heav'n.

Today our Father calls us;
His Holy Spirit waits;
His blessed angels gather
Around the heav'nly gates.
No question will be asked us,
How often we have come;
Although we oft have wandered,
It is our Father's home.

O all-embracing Mercy,
O ever-open Door,
What should we do without you
When heart and eye run o'er?
When all things seem against us,
To drive us to despair,
We know one gate is open,
One ear will hear our prayer.

Lutheran Book of Worship, 304

THIS LITTLE CHILD SAYS YES

The Two Sons and Our Spirituality

Matthew 21:28-32

Helps for Hearing

Think through the cluster of beliefs that make up what we call our "spirituality."

We live by the Spirit, and we walk by the Spirit. *By* Spirit-given faith we accept all that God has done for us in Christ Jesus to give us life. *In* faith we are moved by the Spirit of God to do what God would have us do in worshiping and in helping.

That would be it, except that in the midst of this new life we are yet in the old death. The good the Spirit moves us to do we often do not do; and the evil, which by the Spirit we wish not to do, we often do. That is the evidence of our continuing deadness in the midst of our new life. And so our life in the Spirit must continually be renewed, and our living in the Spirit constantly be reenergized.

And God keeps doing that for us. God's Word through the water of Baptism, through the body and blood of our

WHAT HAPPENED NEXT?

Lord in the Eucharist, and through the law and gospel of the Scriptures deadens death and enlivens life in us.

Through this cluster of beliefs, as through a magnifying lens, we view the source and purpose of our living. We bring them together like the ingredients for making glass, which are then fused and polished into the lens for a telescope. Through that lens we look to God, and through that lens we see how life in the world is to be lived.

That lens, that way of looking at life with God and life with people, is our spirituality. We arrange and emphasize the teachings and beliefs God has given us. We shape our personal theology, and that theology shapes our way of living.

The Lord told the story about the father who one day asked his two sons to go into the vineyard and help with the harvest. The first refused and simply said, "I will not." But later he changed his mind and went to work. The second sounded good as gold. He said, "I go, sir." But he didn't go.

The Lord asked his hearers, "Which of the two did the will of his father?"

In the Gospel according to St. Matthew the application made is that the sinning tax collectors and harlots who repented and accepted Jesus were more obedient to God than the seemingly God-fearing Pharisees and scribes. We could say today that the multitudes of previously pagan peoples in Africa and Asia who are moving into the kingdom are more obedient to God than the peoples of the so-called Christian West.

True enough. But another factor is equally true. Each of us is really two people, two children of God. Sometimes we say "yes" and don't, and sometimes we say "no" and repent and do. We do this double dance time after time. As we see ourselves through the Father's eyes, as we try to understand ourselves and our situation through our cluster of beliefs. What is our view of life lived in the Spirit? What is the controlling view of our spirituality?

This Little Child Says Yes

Through the lens of their spirituality some Christians view the Christian life as a striving more and more to do what the Father wants. Fair enough. This is the will of God—even our sanctification. And much of the will of God can be explained in terms of what we should do and what we should not do. But if what is expected is what we mostly do not produce, and if God is continuously demanding a perfection from us who are inevitably imperfect, who shall deliver us from this deadly situation?

Other Christians, through the lens of their spirituality, see the all-encompassing love of God as the background of the whole picture. God is love. That is God's unique perfection. We can grasp a little of the meaning of that. The mystery of Trinity, one God in three persons, is beyond our grasp, but the essence of the relationship of the three in one must be love. The Father calls Jesus, "My beloved Son." The Son loves the Father. The Spirit must equally be the giver and the receiver of that love. God was in Christ—in all that he did; and the Spirit is in us—in all that is being done—to bring us into that love, to move us to accept that love, and to make us love to be so loved.

The heart of our spirituality, then, is that we accept from the Spirit the forgiving love of God. Of course, we will strive to express our love and follow through in doing, in living the way God would have us live as lovingly as we can. But because our failure to be all even that *we* wish we were, and our failure, even greater, to come anywhere near what *God* would have us be, is so terribly evident, the heart of our spirituality is that we accept the continuing forgiveness of God, that we constantly trust and accept the adopted status that God in Christ has secured for us.

In theological terms, Christian spirituality at its heart is the acceptance of the righteousness that God gives us out of his boundless grace. Without the doubt that thinks it must earn God's love and without the distortion of self-centered remorse which seeks worthiness in regret, we accept the

WHAT HAPPENED NEXT?

Spirit's freely-given forgiveness and the chance to turn again, to begin anew.

In Luther's terms, each one of us is two children, one of whom is named Saint and the other, Sinner. And the heart of the vineyard work that the Father most wants us to do is to repent and believe the gospel.

The rest of the story is told by one of the biblical sons, now grown older, and himself a father.

The Rest of the Story

So often I remember it. For that matter, so often I have done it, over and over again. But I remember that particular time most vividly each year on the evening before the first day of harvest. Even as I say that, I realize that the same recollection colors all the other times in which I manage to be just as foolish, in which I miss the chance to do the good thing I really want to do. Do you know the feeling? No matter what, you can never undo what you did nor ever make up for what you didn't do.

But back to the evening before the first harvest. It was years ago, of course, and because I've done much the same thing again and again over the years, I may confuse some of the details. But that might make it easier for *you* to fit in details you remember of the times *you've* done something similar.

This I remember all too clearly: the word reached us from father—along with all the servants—that the next morning the harvest would begin. The grapes were at their peak. It was *the* time for harvest. We had had exactly the right amount of rain and sun, and the grapes were bursting, luscious. The weather was just right for harvesting. In fact, any grapes we didn't manage to bring in during the next few days would be ruined.

My brother and I were very close. All our lives we had been practically the other's twin, each an alter ego. We were not twins in *fact,* but we certainly were in *act.*

This Little Child Says Yes

This time we reacted in totally different ways. But afterwards, when we compared how we felt, we had both experienced the same dreadful letdown. We had done what we really didn't mean to and had not done what we really wished we would have. You know the feeling?

But back to that evening. Father came into my room and said, "Son, go and work in the vineyard first thing tomorrow morning. This is it! The grapes are bursting. It's just the right time." He went on about how this was the payoff for all the vineyard work, the climax we'd all been waiting for.

I interrupted. I said, "No!" Even now I can hardly believe it was I who said it. Father had said, "Go work in the vineyard," and I said, "I will not." Just like that, not accenting the "I," but of course meaning it, not bearing down on the "will" as if it were a contest between us as to whether I would or wouldn't, and not strong on the "not" as if I had given it a great deal of thought and had made a decision for good reason not to. No. What I said—and you've got to hear the inflection—what I said was in the most supercilious, the most derisive, the most egotistic tone. I said, "I will not" as if it were totally impertinent that my father should even think it at all a possibility that I, the son of a prominent landowner, the coheir with my brother of acres of vineyards and houses and lands—all of that—should be expected to do common labor. The servants, the field hands, *they* did that kind of work. "I will not!" That's what I said.

Perhaps you can tell how the memory makes me blush. Even now, as I tell you about it, I feel like a fool. This was my father asking me to help. I was nothing except for my father. He was the one who gave me life, and without him and my mother I had no being. All those things that I claimed as mine, that made me so arrogant, so turned in on myself, were really his. He did not get those callused hands for doing nothing. He had built up the whole place by his vision and his struggle, and it was his. How could I take that tone over against my father?

If I didn't sense the truth of the matter, my father did. I can still remember his face. His jaw dropped. His mouth opened in astonishment, and then I could see what now I know was a righteous wrath beginning to build. But then his whole face went pale. His forehead and there around his eyes the skin wrinkled in the kind of pain that foretells tears. He turned away and went out the door, shutting it very quietly behind him. Outside in the hall he held on to the doorknob for a few moments. I could tell he was still there, and I found myself looking for a place to hide. Then he dropped his hand and walked quietly away.

Well, I want to say—I guess you know—it was terrible. Mostly it was terrible because what was wrong about the whole business, what was wrong about what I had done, was so clear. It was not merely that I had said I would not help harvest the grapes. That would have meant a difference in the total harvest of about 15 bushels, the way I worked. No, the issue was clear. What was wrong was that I had rejected all the love and care, all the father-child relationship, all that he had slaved to put on the table for me to stuff myself with, all the clothes with which he had kept me warm over the years and made me able to stand with friends as a person of reputation and charm. What was wrong was that I had rejected *him*. I was a fool.

Afterward, I repented and went. I'm glad about that. It was certainly better than not going. I guess everyone would agree that repenting and going is more nearly doing the will of my father than saying no and not going. But I couldn't make up for that no. I couldn't undo it. Fifteen bushels, and what do I get? Even more ashamed and deeper in debt. There was no way, I realized. Were I to work from sunup to sundown, without stopping to rest, without a pause for a drink in the shade, not even if I managed 25 bushels, more than any field hand had managed in one day—there was no way that I could undo what I had done. I had as much as told my father that he was no father of mine and I was no son of his, no child of the family. And I couldn't remove the act and the assinine attitude by saying "I'm sorry" or by sending him a Father's Day card or by "doing better next time."

The only way the break could be healed would be if *he* took the hurt of it all into himself, if he were to bear it, refuse to permit my breaking the father-child relationship, if he were to let the whole ugly incident die inside him and rise up smiling, still loving me in spite of the pain; not just saying, "It was nothing"—because it was everything I have said it was—but saying, "I forgive you."

I've told you my brother and I were almost like twins. This time he went another direction. But in the end, we discovered, we wound up in the same dead end.

(Strange thing! I've been wondering whom you remind me of. It's my brother. You *seem* like him. It's not so much looks or size or male or female. You *seem* like him. Maybe it's because I've felt you being kind of superior, your eyebrows rising as if *you* would never have said, "I will not." It's almost like having my brother here. Well, no matter; whether in the flesh or out of the flesh, I suspect there's no rivalry here among any of us. It's happened to us all.)

My brother told me about it later on. The situation was much the same. He was lying on his bed when the door of the room opened, and there was father saying, "Son, go and work in the vineyard—tomorrow morning, first thing." And the answer? Listen to it. My brother told me about it, described himself, clearly feeling as bad about himself as I had felt.

"Mealymouthed, prissy prig! Goody Two Shoes! That's what I was. 'I go, sir,' I said. I didn't feel that way about myself at the time. I really meant to go, and I was going for the right reason. I loved father, and surely he had the right to ask me to help. But then afterwards, that's when I was

WHAT HAPPENED NEXT?

disgusted with myself and the easy way I said, 'I go, sir.' I didn't go. I slept in. Not 'overslept.' No, I slept in, deliberately, knowing the choice I was making. I knew I was going to ignore the alarm clock's warning that it was high time to wake out of sleep."

That's the way my brother described it. I could feel for him. You too? Do we all remember times when we said, "I will" and really meant it, but then we didn't go? That is the bottom line. And it tells us more than that we have been fools. It says we're not in control of ourselves. We can't even follow through on what we will to do.

My brother and I agreed that my repenting and going was in some ways closer to doing what father wanted than my brother's saying he would and then not doing so. But it was the way he felt about it afterwards that made me realize how twin-like we were, my brother and I. He said, "I felt awful. I could remember father's warm smile and how he nodded his head and said, 'Get some sleep,' and quietly closed the door. And then, when they told me and I came running out to the vineyard I knew it was too late, that I could never make up for it, never undo it. I wept then, and I've wept bitterly many times since, remembering it."

But that's a part of the story you may not know—what happened afterwards. I had finally got to work, and the foreman credited me with quite a few bushels, but there were as many tears as drops of sweat I wiped away as I thought of what I'd said, what I'd done to father. It must have been just then that father realized that my brother was not working, had not showed up at all, and didn't intend to. Because he stood up very deliberately, left the record book open on the stand in the shade by the side of the field, pulled on his gloves, and walked out into the burden and heat of the day and began to load up the baskets of grapes and carry them to the winepress alone.

I didn't see him when he was stricken. But there was a sudden hush over the field as if every living thing was

This Little Child Says Yes

holding its breath, and then people running to the edge of the field where the winepress was. And I *knew*—somehow I knew—it was father, his heart.

"Oh, my father, my father!" That's what my brother said when a servant rushed up to his room to tell him of father's heart attack. With tears streaming down his cheeks, he said, "Would God I had died for you! No! Would God that I had done what I said!"

And that's the way I felt too, when I reached father. At least I was there, able to tell father how I felt. I fell on my knees where he lay on the ground and put his head into my lap, and said, "Father, I have sinned. Would God that I had never said what I did."

And then father opened his eyes, his hand moved just a little to press mine, he looked up at me, smiled just a little, and said, "Remember, I love you." That was it. No rebuke. Not "That's all right." It was, "Remember, I love you. You know that. And I know you love me. Nothing can separate us, not angels nor principalities nor powers, nor things present nor things to come, not things we've done in life, not death—nothing! Tell your brother that too—tell him from me. Nothing can separate us."

And he died.

It is true. Nothing can separate us. And both of us—can I say *all* of us—are closer now after his death than ever we were before. It is as if his death gave us new life. Weeping? Yes, we're never quite done with that, no more than we are done with our saying "no" and then having to repent and saying "yes" and not doing. It would be great if we could say "yes" all the time and *do!*

That's what I tell my children. Here I am now after these years with these two twins. "A saint and a sinner," I tell them, sometimes one, sometimes the other. Hard to tell them apart. My children do the yes and the no routine, too. And I try to help them see that saying yes and doing is the happy way, is real living.

WHAT HAPPENED NEXT?

I began it with that little child's play—you know it:

This little pig went to market.
This little pig stayed home.
This little pig had roast beef.
This little pig had none.
This little pig cried WEE *all the way home.*

It doesn't say much. Just counts out five toes. Of course, they loved it, laughed at it. But when they would quiet down I'd add a little comment—after all, *oui* is "yes" in French, isn't it?

This little child went to market.
(And you may grow up to be a big merchant or a seller of stocks and a buyer of bonds.)

This little child stayed home.
(And you may be a housekeeper or even a shut-in who can never get out of the house at all.)

This little child had roast beef.
(And you may have good things to eat, house, home, spouse, children, good friends, faithful neighbors.)

This little child had none.
(And you may be left hungry and poor and alone.)

But this little child said yes all the way home!
They soon learned it, that last line. They'd chime in eagerly at the end—or sleepily if my sermon had been too long—"This little child said yes all the way home!"

We add new meanings to that yes as we grow older, as we repeat the saint and sinner roles. I hope both will learn and remember that it is not only the yes and the doing that are the important things—if they were, who shall stand?

Even more important:

This little child says, "Yes, the Father's love is greater than all my nos."

This little child says, "Yes, the Father forgives and I can start all over anew."

This Little Child Says Yes

This little child says, "Yes, it is true: nothing can separate us from the love of God in Christ Jesus."

It is his yes that takes us all the way home!

sanctification
doing in remembrance

GETTING BACK INTO THE VINEYARD AFTER THE PAYOFF OF GRACE

The Prodigal Son, The Well-paid Laborers, The Emmaus Pilgrims

Matthew 20:1-16
Luke 15:11-24
Luke 24:13-35

Helps for Hearing

How do we manage to control ourselves—for goodness' sake?

How do we live, more and more, the way we want to live—for God's sake?

It's sanctification we're asking about. It's about being made holy, but it's also about doing what is right and good and loving. In one sense sanctification is completely God's action. In spite of our disobedience, God forgives us and accepts us as though we were not sinners at all, but as holy, as sanctified. That sanctification is revealed to us and made our own through all that God has done for us in Jesus Christ. That meaning of sanctification includes all that the loving God has done to make us acceptable.

In another sense sanctification includes our action. God moves us by the Holy Spirit "both to will and to do" things that are holy. That meaning of sanctification includes all the holy living we do and all the growing in holy living we can aspire to.

What we want to know is, after we have been made holy in God's sight by grace, how do we manage more and more to live in holiness? We want not only to know that, but to do it.

Our doing good and our improving in holy living depends on our will, on our wanting. How do we control our wills so that we want to do what is pleasing to God and want *not* to do what displeases God?

Even our sanctified will is not the whole of it, of course. St. Paul complained that he really did want to do the good, but all too often failed to go beyond willing to doing. But still our will is the origin of our action. And back of our will to do one specific thing is our will that *wants* to want to do the good.

It is God who makes us both to will and to do. How does God get at us for goodness' sake?

Use your head, for goodness' sake. There is a lot to that, of course. Doing what is good does in many ways pay off with good returns. Thinking things through clearly can result in sensible action, and what makes sense is often good. Thinking and willing are related. But thinking about what? Comparing values? The prodigal son putting pigs and pods in one pan of the scale and "the bread and to spare" which his father's servants had in the other—did that result in his going home? That approach seems to suggest that what's good for me is *good*. Will that enable us to fit into God's idea of what is good? Part of the problem is that our judgment might still rate the fun of riotous living as worth the cost of the pigs and pods. Even our head must be under the Spirit's power, must be able to make good judgments, before it can safely be used.

Christians believe that God was in Christ and Christ Jesus was with us in our time and did what needed to be done to enable us to know the good, to will it, and to do it. Jesus is both the model of the godly life and the sacrifice for our sin, for our not living the godly life. As we observe how Jesus Christ lived, we teach our heads.

But how about our willing and our doing? These need changing, sanctifying. There must be more to remembering than merely recalling. Jesus is the Word in flesh. And what he did was the Word in action. What is written of what he did is the Word in print. And when we remember what is written, when we bring to our minds all that he did, the Word is at work in us to change our minds from evil and move our wills to *want* and our selves to *do* the good. "Keep in mind," the canticle sings, "that Jesus Christ has died for us and is risen from the dead" (*Lutheran Book of Worship*, 13). As we remember that, we use our heads to change and to control our wills.

Is not that what our Lord intended us to do as we celebrate his Supper? Eat, drink, "in remembrance of me." We love God because he first loved us and gave himself for us in his Son, Jesus. We keep on loving God by remembering how he first loved us and gave himself for us. Since love is the fulfilling of the law, and since our love grows out of God's love, it is by our remembering what God did that we bring the power of the Spirit to direct what we do.

Remember that for goodness' sake.

The Rest of the Story

It's a pub, a Palestinian pub. Imagine the vintner behind the bar dispensing the fruit of the vine but serving, as well, as confidant and adviser.

WHAT HAPPENED NEXT?

A young man comes in, ring on his finger, expensive-looking robe, new sandals. He's obviously been celebrating, but one wouldn't describe him as high, rather somewhat low after a high. He looks troubled, concerned, perhaps uncertain.

The vintner speaks: "Good to see you. Been a long time. Heard you'd struck out on your own, gone off to the far country. What'll it be?"

The young man replies: "Just got back, this afternoon in fact. Make it a glass of chablis."

The vintner pours and then moves off down the bar to serve other customers. After a bit he drifts back, partly out of curiosity, partly aware of the young man's dis-ease. He stands just to the left of the glass of chablis and expresses his willingness to listen by a slow wiping and polishing of the bar. It is enough. The vintner hears it all, first in fits and starts, but then in a flood.

Strangely it all begins with, "My father was waiting for me! While I was yet a great way off, my father . . . " and then a pause and a shaking of his head. Then it all comes out, how his father had given him his share of the estate, how he had set out for the far country. "I had a ball, I tell you!" The words come through a little defensively. How after a few weeks, the money gone and the fair-weather friends with it, he'd ended up working for a farmer, a pig farmer. "It was pretty rough. Funny thing, I kept thinking of bread, of all the food here at home at the farm. Even the servants have more than enough, and I was perishing for hunger. So I came back, ready to make a clean breast of it, admit I'd made a fool of myself and ask to be taken on as one of the hired servants. And then—and this is the strangest part—while I was yet a great way off, my father . . . ." He pauses, and his voice is rough with emotion, "he had been waiting for me, as though he was expecting me, looking down the road for me. While I was yet a great way off, my father came

Getting Back into the Vineyard After the Payoff of Grace

running toward me and threw his arms around me and kissed me.

"I got started on my confession," the young man goes on, " 'Father, I have sinned against heaven and before you,' and was going on with it, but he paid no attention. He called for the house servants. He sent one back into the house to get this robe and this ring and these sandals, sent another out to prepare the fatted calf, and set up a banquet. And what he said then! 'My son was dead, and is alive again; he was lost, and is found.' It was a fact, too. I was half dead, and I've certainly found out that what I had here was better than what I left back there."

The bar had probably never been wiped drier, but the vintner didn't have to say anything to keep the story going.

"It was a great party. What a spread! Music and dancing. Just broke up an hour or so ago."

The vintner, smiling, filled the young man's glass again. "On the house," he says, shaking his head as the young man reaches for a coin. "On the house. Welcome home. Sounds like you've got it made." A pause and then: "Why the long face?" The vintner's tone is friendly but the overtones imply, "Get to the problem."

"No problem," the young man says. "Things are great." But his voice trails off, and there is no smile on his face.

The vintner's bar cloth suddenly reverses its motion and begins to move down the bar. The message was clear: "Your hour is almost up. I've got other customers too. They've all got problems."

Suddenly the young man looks up right into the vintner's eyes. "It's tomorrow morning! That's the problem! How do I manage tomorrow morning? They're well into the plowing. I saw the plow standing waiting at the end of a furrow. Plowing around and around the field, the plowshare biting off just a foot from the four edges each time around. Plowing—on and on forever. I hate it! That's one of the reasons I left."

39

WHAT HAPPENED NEXT?

Again his voice trails off. "And it was great while it lasted." And then softly, "While I was yet a great way off, my father.... But tomorrow, how do I manage to wake up and get up and go out and start out ... plowing?"

"Well," the vintner says, "think about what a waste it all was—money gone, friends forsook you. Think of the pigs, for goodness' sake."

"But that doesn't do it," the young man interrupts. "I've tried that, tried reminding myself of how bad it was. The trouble is it was a *riot* before that. I've never had so much fun. No, remembering the bad and the worst of it doesn't do it, for goodness' sake. I still find myself longing for the far country."

Now the vintner has had it. "But your father ... " he blurts out, hardly a nondirective counselor. "You ought to remember him. He welcomed you back—while you were a long way off. You keep saying so yourself. The ring. The robe. The feast. And—this you ought to know—he really suffered because you'd gone. I used to see him walking down the road here to where the left fork takes off for the far country. His shoulders have sagged. You must have seen how white his hair has turned. I'd say he's aged 30 years, suffered hell for you, for goodness' sake. Just think about that. Just remember that. That ought to get you going, for goodness' sake."

The vintner ends the discussion with a fierce final scrub of an imaginary spot on the bar and moves down to the center. Three men have just come in, laughing and nodding their heads at one another, plunking down silver coins on the bar. They can't wait to tell their story more than they can't wait for a drink.

"Guess what happened?"—and they wait for no guess. "We just got paid a day's wage for working in the vineyard one hour."

"How'd you manage that?" The vintner knew the straight man's line.

Getting Back into the Vineyard After the Payoff of Grace

The story comes out from the trio, how they had drifted in and out of the marketplace all day, half hoping to be hired and half hoping not to be. The times they were in the market checking, no one was hiring.

Then finally at five o'clock they were in the market once more, and a man who owned a vineyard came by. "Why aren't you working?" he asked.

"No one has hired us."

"Well, go into my vineyard and work."

And so they did. After an hour it was time to quit. They were paid first—and got a whole day's wages. At first they thought it was a mistake, and they were ready to pocket the money and run. But that didn't seem right, so they hung around until the other workers were paid.

"You should have heard the fuss. They had seen how much we had been paid, so they expected more because they had worked all day. But the owner said, 'I haven't cheated you. You agreed to a day's work for a silver coin. And that's what you got. Take your pay and go home. Are you jealous because I am generous?'

"It didn't seem fair to us either, of course, but we were not complaining. After everyone else had gone home still muttering, we went up to the owner once again and thanked him. He sort of waved aside our thanks and then—it was really a surprise—he said he'd been watching us work and said that we could be about the best workers of the lot. He said—and we had to admit it was true—we didn't seem to know much about grapes, but that he was sure he could turn us into first-class vinedressers. Kind of set us up! 'Come out early tomorrow, and follow me, and I will make pickers of you men.'"

There is a pause. A silence settles over the pub. Then slowly one of the men says, "Maybe that's just what it was—a setup. He's trying to hook us. I'm not so sure I want to get out there at 6 A.M. and bear the burden and heat of the day, for goodness' sake. We could show up again at five in the afternoon and get paid just as much."

This is evidently more than the vintner can take. He's had it. He bursts out, "Oh, for goodness' sake. Yours was a payoff of grace. You admit it yourselves. And now you're thinking of holding him up? Think about what he said! He'll make you into first-class vinedressers. He's already started to change you. You came in here with more energy and more purpose and more joy than I've ever seen you show. When the sun comes up tomorrow morning, remember what he said, for goodness' sake. And remember what he did—paid you a whole day's wage. But remember most— he's already changed you. You're different men. Remember that, for goodness' sake."

How it all would have turned out is not clear, because suddenly two men push open the door, their faces lit up as if they had seen the most amazing sight in the world. They both begin to talk at once, and they interrupt one another and laugh and race on to get the story out.

"You know that man who we hoped would liberate Israel, that Jesus who preached that the kingdom of God is at hand ... ?"

"The one whom the Romans crucified Friday?"

"Of course," says the vintner. "He died, right? Nicodemus and some of his servants managed to get Pilate's permission to take his body down and bury it. In Joseph's tomb. Some of the men stopped in here after. They rolled a great stone in front of the grave."

"He's alive!" It comes out as a duet, a double shout. "Jesus is alive again!"

And then words come tumbling out from both of them. About how they had been slowly walking from Jerusalem to Emmaus discouraged and downhearted at making the trip with all their hope gone, when suddenly a man appeared and joined them. How he at first seemed to know nothing about Jesus and what had happened, what he had preached,

Getting Back into the Vineyard After the Payoff of Grace

and the miracles he had performed and how he had been arrested and crucified—but then suddenly he had said, "Oh foolish men and slow of heart to believe all that the prophets have spoken!" How he had rehearsed all the plan of God's salvation from Moses through the prophets. And how all of a sudden it was very clear: all that had happened to Jesus was by God's plan. It was God bringing salvation to Israel—and to all who will believe!

And that wasn't all. The man had agreed to stay with them at their house in Emmaus because evening had come. When they sat down to supper, he took the bread from the plate, gave thanks to God, and, as he broke it, suddenly they knew! It was Jesus. He was alive!

They shout it. "It is Jesus! He's alive!" They jump up and down in their excitement.

The vintner is cautious. "Alive? If he's alive and down in Emmaus, what are you doing here back at Jerusalem?"

"We came back to tell his disciples, and they knew it already! Some of the women had been at the grave and found it empty, and Mary had seen him and talked with him in the garden near the tomb. Anyway, Jesus disappeared from our house just as we recognized him in the act of breaking the bread.

"Isn't it amazing? This makes all the difference in the world. Think about it. It does make everything different. He was dead, and now he came back to life again. He must be, just as he said, the Son of God. Remember how at the grave of Lazarus he said that whoever lives and believes in him will never die? If you know that, your whole life is different.

"We were disappointed at first—Jesus disappearing just when we came to recognize him. But then we realized that being able to see him is not as important as knowing he is alive, knowing that he is the Messiah. We were a bit irritated at first when we got to Jerusalem and found that everybody already knew. That long trip for nothing! Except for sharing the joy of it, what difference did it make?

WHAT HAPPENED NEXT?

"We're really commuting today. We're going back to Emmaus to make sure they all know back there. We used to complain about that trip back and forth. But not tonight! He's alive. Every day, every trip, everything ought to be different now, just remembering what that all means!

"It makes all the difference, for goodness' sake!"

And to all who believe, to all of us today, it makes all the difference for goodness' sake. Jesus lives. What he came to do, what he did, to show us, to save us, to change us, he is still doing, still doing inside our very beings. He shapes our wills; he moves us to do. He clearly doesn't force us, but he says, "Come to me! Follow me! Remember! Just think!" Who can forget it, ever? To all who bring to mind the Christ who is alive, to all who remember the love that reached us in our far country, to all who day after day receive the payoff of grace, it makes all the difference for goodness' sake. To us all he gives power to be, and more and more to become, the children of God.

Those who remember can set their hands to their plows on Monday mornings, can get out to the vineyard as the dawn breaks, and can keep traveling until journey's end.

Remember—for goodness' sake!

absolution
the service and the communion

LET'S DO IT AGAIN

The Paralyzed Man and the Liturgy

Mark 2:1-12

Helps for Hearing

"It's like running around in circles," some would say.

"That's the way most races are run—and won," could be the reply.

There *are* circles within the circle of the Christian's weekly round. And as we run each of them, an uninvolved observer could say, "You're not getting anywhere."

Each week we confess we are sinners, we are still in bondage to the power of sin, and we have committed specific sins. We receive forgiveness of sin and then go home to sin again for a week. The next Sunday we complete the absolution circle by coming around again for forgiveness.

Each week we come to be built up by the Word of God. Our foundations are strengthened through the Word in the lessons. Our spirits are lifted by the Word in hymns and liturgy. Sermon after sermon supplies the Word like building blocks. The Word through the community changes the structure to a living space. Then the wear and tear of the week makes it necessary to renovate and repair on the next Sunday.

Each week the Word in the sacrament brings power into our living, but the service man must come regularly or nothing works right.

The non-Christian might comment, "What's the point? If you could see some improvement and could hope finally to be O.K., then perhaps there would be some purpose to it all." Or another might say, "If you wouldn't dwell on it so. Of course, we aren't perfect. Why keep examining your mistakes? Why not emphasize the positive? You do what you can. Who can expect more?"

Not every Christian has it all straight, and whole centuries of Christian practice have experienced distorted rounds of the church's doing of the liturgy. It could help us to think through again why it is that week after week we gather together and do those circle dances we call the liturgy.

A sober diagnosis of our illness is basic. We are sick of sin. Like diabetes, if we have it, we have it. It's not like being pregnant. One can be a little bit diabetic as compared with having a severe diabetic condition. But once you have it, there's no going back to not having it. It doesn't go away. You have it, you keep it, and you tend it, or else the complications are to be dreaded and are finally deadly.

But since 1920—since a specific time in history—there is insulin. (For insulin think salvation, life, forgiveness. Think God's Old Testament acts, God's action in the fullness of time, all God is even now doing. Think the Word, the Scriptures, the sacraments, the community, worship.) Insulin must be injected. A hypodermic needle must be filled and the point thrust through the skin and the insulin shot into the system. Over and over, day after day, going around in circles and not getting anywhere—unless being *alive* is anything, unless being with loved ones, doing one's life's work, sharing in the wonders and possibilities of this universe—

unless these things count. There is no improvement—not in the sense of a cure—and one does have to concentrate on the problem in order to use the solution and experience the blessings. But that being done, it is the next best thing to never having been ill at all.

In some sense, having diabetes is terribly serious, the whole repeated cycle of blood tests and injections a matter of life over against death. In some sense, it is a monstrous chore one would like to have done with, or it can become so habitual one scarcely gives it a second thought. In some sense, the repeated miracle of receiving insulin is the most joyful, most thrilling, most vital experience in existence. It means giving yourself life and loving and achieving and knowing and sensing. It means *being* over against a repeated daily danger of *not being*.

In a similar sense, for the person who has Christianity, going the repeated circles within the liturgy and in the whole round of the church year means life itself, real living. It means God's loving and loving God. It means adoption as God's children. It means the close friendship of the Son and the comfort of the Holy Spirit. It means the injection of God's mysterious grace and the reception of the body and the blood of the Savior. It means the indwelling of the Trinity. It reverses death and then holds it at bay and finally is death's conqueror. It means life here. It means life everlasting.

It also demands time and interrupts our doing other things we'd like to do. It can also be a chore, and it can become mere habit. It would be a pity if we were to forget and become used to the miracles that repeatedly happen when we go to church.

All of this is why Christians are glad when they hear it said unto them, "Let us go unto the house of the Lord." And when they have done their liturgy, you can hear them say—not right away perhaps, but in a week: "Let's do it again!"

The Rest of the Story

Sit over here on this bench. Now you can see. There, across the traffic of Twelfth Street to that fairly new building

WHAT HAPPENED NEXT?

right across, the one with the flat facade, strips of wide windows running down from the roof to the sidewalk with flat marble facing in between. There must be 13 floors.

Now, see that rope dangling over the cornice at the roof's edge? Follow it down along the first row of windows. See the man dangling on the end of the rope? Not really dangling—see, he gives a tug to the rope, and he moves down to the window below him. He must be in a sort of chair, suspended by several ropes. He has a bucket with a sponge. He gives a quick wash to the window and then dries it with one of those rubber squeegees. Then another tug on the rope. He lowers himself to the next window and does it all over again.

Watch. What will happen after he finishes the last window, just above the sidewalk level? A final tug, his feet on the sidewalk, he puts his squeegee in the pail and the pail on his arm. Releasing his chair, he carries it all to the front door of the building and goes in. Now, how long will it take? An elevator to the top floor, an iron stairway, perhaps, up to the roof door, out onto the tar and gravel, and over to the front edge of the building.

Sure enough, his head and shoulders appear, the rope is flipped and tugged over to center on the next shaft of windows. Somehow he attaches the chair and the pail. Now he's climbed over and is on his way to the top window, doing it all over again.

Be aware now. Something is about to happen. We'll be a part of it, but at the same time we'll be standing apart, watching it happen. The rush of cars runs out at both ends of the street, and it is suddenly quiet. The street itself narrows to a cart's width, the asphalt crumbling into dirt and gravel. The 13 floors seem to telescope into one another until there is only a one-story building, a whitewashed stone house, in its place. There is a narrow stairs that climbs up one side of the building to the flat roof. It's evidently used as a veranda

Let's Do It Again

where the family can gather after the fierce sun has set to enjoy the cool evening breeze.

Four people come around the house at the far end of the street and then, following them, many more. Soon the road in front of the house is crowded with an eager, bustling, buzzing crowd. They're all dressed like people in an illustrated Bible story book. The first group of four moves into the house as the door is opened, followed by more and more others, until clearly there is room for no more. On the street outside there is standing room only.

Shift down the road a bit, and look down the side street. A strange clutch of people is coming, four men carrying a litter supported on two poles. A fifth man is lying on a sort of mat which has been laid on the stretcher that the four are carrying. They stop at the sight of the crowd, lower the litter to the ground, and straighten up, as much in surprise and disappointment as for rest. It is clear they had intended to carry the man into the house. Now they realize they are completely blocked even from the doorway, with no hope of getting in.

There is a major consultation, the four bearers explaining the situation to the man on the litter. He is clearly not able to do much of anything for himself. He hasn't turned his head or tried to roll over on his elbow to be in a position to see. And small as his bedridden profile is, it seems to shrink in disappointment as the problem is explained.

But then one bearer seems to make an animated suggestion. A buzz goes back and forth. The bearer runs off to a house down the road and returns with two coils of rope. There is a great deal of gesturing and trial grasping of the stretcher before the four do a *one-two-three* and lift the man, carrying him to the narrow stairs at the side of the house. They heave and hoist, trying to keep the stretcher level as they move up the stairs, until finally they set the bed carefully on the tiles of the roof.

WHAT HAPPENED NEXT?

We're all aware—we've known all along—why there is such a crowd and who is in the house. It is Jesus Christ. The four friends want to bring the sick man to him for healing. We know it is the paralyzed man, and, sure enough, what we know is about to happen does happen. The four men begin to take up the tiles from the roof at a measured distance from the front and side. They break through into the room below. There is a pushing and shoving out the door as some of the crowd pull away from the dirt and clutter falling from the ceiling. Angry voices are raised, aimed at the men on the roof. They pay no attention, but stretch the ropes taut over the opening they have made, balance the mattress and the paralytic on the ropes, and begin slowly to lower their burden. They are directly above the Son of God. He is brushing plaster and caulking from his shoulders and hair.

We can all crowd around now, here on the roof, and look down. We know what will be said, as if we had memorized the characters' lines, and we know what will happen. Jesus will heal him. But before that he will tell him his sin is forgiven. What really is the man's problem? Yes, he is paralyzed. But what is *wrong* with him? Will Jesus merely be role playing with him when he is lying at his feet? Will he merely be getting at his critics when he says, "My son, your sins are forgiven"?

Can we imagine what is wrong with him? Put yourself in his position. Think his thoughts with him as he moves down the six feet and through fewer seconds before he must appear before the Son of God. "Here consider your station according to the Ten Commandments," the Catechism's instruction on confession tells us. Do you fear and love God above all things—or in your paralysis have you cursed God and hoped to die? Have you blamed it all on your parents? Have you taken it out on your wife and children? Have you been a terrible grouch with your neighbors? Have you filled in the long hours with gossip or even slander, all the time

Let's Do It Again

coveting the better lot of others? Most of all, have you anguished over the awful fact that even though you wanted to want whatever is good and beautiful and true, you found yourself in the death grip of a will that wanted really all that was evil and opposite? And now do you find yourself flat on your back before the Son of God, unable even to kneel and cry, "Lord, have mercy"?

Then you know the overwhelming joy of seeing the Lord's kind look and hearing the Lord's strong words, "Be of good cheer! Your sins are forgiven!" All the rest of it—the argument about "who can forgive sins but God alone?" ... the proof of the promise in the command, "Rise up, take up your bed and walk" ... the flood of strength and feeling of well-being rushing through your whole body ... actually doing it, sitting up, leaning forward, getting your weight centered over your heels and then standing, and stretching out your arms to Jesus ... and then stooping down, rolling up the mat and walking out the door—all of that happens and it is all miracle, but it takes second place to hearing in his own voice, seeing in his eyes, "Son, your sins are forgiven!" Good cheer! Three good cheers!

"Take up your bed and go home." But not yet, not right away. Instead, going around the house to the stairs at the side and climbing up to the roof and grasping the hands of the four friends.

Now hear the healed man say, "Let's do it again!"

The four hear him and laugh and slap his back and hug him. But he halfway means it. He sees the Lord standing there still looking up through the hole in the roof. The healed and forgiven one would rather be there by the side of the Lord than anywhere. And returning now the look of the Lord, he moves his lips to say "Thank you!" The Lord Jesus waves a hand, and the words can be read on his lips, "Go in peace."

Perhaps that's not what happened next. But from where we are standing, we can see not only down the narrow street to the unparalyzed man's home, but into the next weeks of his life. Everything is wonderful at first, everyone at home and all the neighbors welcoming him and marveling at how he can walk. But soon, for everyone but him, it begins to hang out. The street is always jammed with sightseers, and the neighbors can't find a place to park. The man practically holds court. He tells the story over and over again until everyone else is weary of hearing about it. And one morning his wife shrills, "Are you going to spend the rest of your life bragging about it? Why don't you go out and get a job? I'm sick and tired of having you underfoot around the house all day."

He is not so much surprised as angry, and not so much angry as ashamed, and so he covers up with angry answers. But he doesn't know what he can do, and there aren't many jobs to be had, and he's ashamed of how much *he* has been the center of his repeated story and how little Jesus has figured in. And, although he had intended to, he never did go back to find Jesus and thank him again, hadn't really done much about Yahweh either after all those years of promises about what he would do and what he would be like if only he could get around again. Even while he knew he was at fault and was ashamed because he was, he barked at one child and cuffed another as he stormed out of the house, and he kicked the dog and knew he was a poor, miserable sinner.

When he came to himself—that is, when the Spirit helped him sort it all out—he went looking for his four friends. And when he found them, he said, "Let's do it again." And this time they could tell he really meant it. "Go with me again. Let me down again, just as I am, before the Lord, so that I can hear him say again, 'Be of good cheer. Your sins are forgiven.' Let's do it again."

Isn't all this just the way it is with all of us here? "My daughter, be of good cheer. Your sins are forgiven. My son, be of good cheer. Here is forgiveness and your mat and your

Let's Do It Again

health and your home and your wife and your children, your dog, your work and the kingdom and life everlasting and your—everything. Why aren't you of good cheer? Why isn't your life different, and why are you still so selfish and so self-centered? Do you need to be forgiven again—and again? Do you need a new start again and again, be filled with new strength again and again? Let's do it again.

The old Palestinian buildings have disappeared, and we are back at the window washer's building. Thirteen floors from the roof to where we can get our feet on the ground once more. Take the elevator—and hear what is in store for you at each stop as the days and the weeks and the years go by.

13th Floor: making a living, the mortgage, the kids' education, college.

12th Floor: tonsils, broken arms, the dentist, arthritis, Alzheimer's disease.

11th Floor: the neighbors, the nation, the world, the bomb, starvation in Africa.

10th Floor: second-hand goods—all the good resolutions never kept, dreams of what might have been, and regrets that they haven't.

9th Floor: Baptism's covenant and confirmation promises and vows.

8th Floor: all we could have done for one another and haven't, all the things we never intended to do to one another but have.

7th Floor: what I've done that you'd never guess and all the things you remember all too well.

6th Floor: God's tears, as God, like a hen gathering her chicks under her wings, calls us, and we would not.

5th Floor: shelves full of years remaining, lined with boxes of weeks, filled with individually wrapped days.

4th Floor: walls and walls of photographs of the people you know who look to you in love and in longing.

WHAT HAPPENED NEXT?

3rd Floor: mirrors, large and small, each one reflecting what you are thinking and resolving right now.

2nd Floor: the other side of the mirrors reflecting the person sitting next to you or the one you wish were there.

1st Floor: death—the end and the beginning.

Here, our feet on the floor, say it: "Let's do it again. Let's return again, turn again, and ask for our Lord's, 'Be of good cheer. Your sins are forgiven!' "

As we say it, the Spirit of God catches us up and carries us with millions of others high above all the churches of the world. Their roofs open up to our sight, and we see crowds pushing in at all the doors softly saying, "Let's do it again." They push into the Presence, and we, too, find ourselves in our place in our church, kneeling at his feet, the Son of Man, clothed with a long robe and with a golden girdle round his breast. The hair of his head is white as snow-white wool, and his eyes flame like fire. His feet gleam like burnished brass, and his voice is like the sound of rushing waters. And he says, "Fear not, I am the first and the last, and the living one; I died, and behold I am alive for evermore" (Rev. 1:12-18).

Softly we say, "Do it again." And we hear him saying, "Your sins are forgiven. Be of good cheer. It is I. A spirit has not flesh and blood as you see that I have. Take. Eat. Take. Drink. Take up your days and walk—through the weeks and the years. Come home. Come in peace. Serve the Lord."

There is one great and grateful cry: "Thanks be to God!"

regenerate life

THE DAUGHTER OF JAIRUS RAISED AGAIN

Mark 5:21-24, 35-43

Helps for Hearing

How to get along with a child—that's what this is about. How to get along with a child of God exactly your age, that is the problem. And not just any child your age, but you—just you (or "just-and-unjust-you," "saint-and-sinner-you"). How *you* can best get along with *you,* that child-of-God you.

Almost certainly our minds are adding to the question "... when we are bad, when we fail, when we act like people still dead-in-sin." But we may need to focus even more on how we get along with our "raised-to-new-life" self. That is who we actually are. The question is, "How do we get along with our 'selfs' that have been raised from the dead to newness of life?" Often our problem *is* that we are discouraged about our poor performance, and we are critical of ourselves. But aren't we being negative then about the strength of our *new* life? And isn't that being critical of *God*?

There is a maxim for Christian parents that goes like this: remember that your two-year-old is usually acting the way a two-year-old baptized child of God is expected to act.

WHAT HAPPENED NEXT?

Whether your resurrection to new life in Baptism is two years, 20, or 50 years old, ought we not share God's expectations of how we will act, and not expect more of ourselves than God expects?

This is not to say that what we do is always what God would hope we would do, nor what in his holiness he urges us to do. It means that what we do does not surprise God. God knows us, our weaknesses and our strengths. He gave us our life. He raised us to new life. He knows that we died in sinning, and how strong the pull of that death is. But the new life we have is God's life in us. Surely God also knows how strong is the resurrection power in us. If God is confident that he can keep doing the good work he has begun in us, ought we not be persuaded even when we experience defeats?

It is obvious to us that we reflect a cracked image of God. We say of a child, "He's the spittin' image of his father." We know that we are the fightin', the covetin', the lustin' image of our great-grandmother Eve and great-grandfather Adam.

But are we equally consistent in realizing we are new persons in Christ? By Holy Baptism's new birth we are new creatures. We have been raised from a death-in-sin to new life-in-Christ. The desires and hopes and dreams and sensory responses we experience continue naturally in our living. They are not themselves bad. They are part of our being human, they are average, they are neutral. What we do about them, with them, because of them, will differ, depending on whether we deal with them as "dead" or as "alive." We can respond in ways distorted and wrong, but our responses can just as possibly be just, just what the Father ordered, just what our Brother reflected, just what the Spirit moves us to do. Our responses can just as possibly reflect our raised-again life, because we are not "more dead than alive."

We hope always to "look alive." We hope for our self to be alive as St. Paul said, "It is no longer I who live, but

The Daughter of Jairus Raised Again

Christ who lives in me" (Gal. 2:20). But realistically we expect our selves to act in a mixed way. We should expect ourselves to act as we do, because we are yet both in death and in life. We should cheer when we move with the Spirit. We should not be surprised nor despondent when our weakness is too strong for us. We *are* the children of God. My self is a child of God. "It does not yet appear what we shall be" (1 John 3:2). We are "on the way." We are original sinners, yes, but equally, even more, we are subsequent saints.

Eventually we shall see God as God is. Meanwhile we should look at God as Jesus revealed him. We have been introduced to God through the Son of God, the Word in flesh. We should be continually introducing God to our self by the Word remembered. Our new life is strengthened in our remembering what, as God-in-Christ, Jesus has done for us, in remembering our baptism in which our new self was raised up, in remembering in the Lord's Supper when our self is fed with the body and blood of the true child, Jesus, our Lord.

Eventually we shall see God as he is. Now we want to keep remembering God as he has revealed himself. The Word will keep raising us to new life again, to life in Christ, so that God can see *us* as he is.

The rest of the story is about the daughter of Jairus. She was 12 years old when she began to live a second time. How did she get along in the new life she led? Did she always expect she would be the way she discovered she was, still partly dead even though made alive? Did she relax in her resurrection, accepting herself as she was? Did her remembering what the Lord had done for her persuade her that he could, that he would, raise her again and again?

The Rest of the Story

It wasn't easy for us to be special—"Peter-James-and-John this" and "Peter-James-and-John that." Of course, we did get special opportunities, and that was good. But, speaking just for my brother James and me—and for our mother—it had its temptations, too. I'm afraid you all know about how we tried to preempt the two seats of honor on the Lord's right and left when he would take over his kingdom. That "special" business made for difficulties with our friends, too. Sometimes the other nine disciples let us have it about being favored. Then, in a perverse sort of way, we sometimes did stupid things—well, actually, *wrong* things—to show we were just like everybody else. Remember, "Shall we call down fire?"

Come to think about it, ours was very much like your situation—being special in an unspecial world, even special among other special people. All too often we fail to *specialize*. Come right down to it, the problem for each one of us is to be special in our "self." We, all of us, have an all-too-average human nature. We think too often of the special part of our self as if it were inside that human nature—just a small spark of life in a mostly dead nature. Isn't it the other way around? Isn't a spark of life much bigger than any sign of death? Do you understand the mix you are? How do you get on with your self? Have you decided which self you really want to be when you say you want to be your self? Do you like your self?

You remember in the Gospel that bears my name—"to all . . . who believed in his name, he gave power to become children of God" (John 1:12). You might think, "If you're someone's child, you *are* a child; you don't have to *become* a child." Well, think about that. The purpose of that Gospel—remember, at the end?—"These are written that you may believe that Jesus is the Christ, the Son of God, and that believing you may have life in his name" (John 20:31). What I'm saying is that, indeed, you do have life now, and you do have the power to live like a child of God—but you are also still becoming. Don't think that you are perfect, or have to be—or that God expects you to be. He *wants* you to be,

The Daughter of Jairus Raised Again

and God's Spirit works at it in you. But God is realistic, and you ought to be too.

That first epistle of the three that bear my name seems to imply more—remember? "No one born of God commits sin; for God's nature abides in him, and he cannot sin because he is born of God" (1 John 3:9). Taken by itself, that can make any one of us who is aware of a double self wonder: "Do I really have the new life in Christ? I keep sinning. I do!" There's an earlier passage which sets the balance: "If we say we have no sin, we deceive ourselves, and the truth is not in us. If we confess our sins, he is faithful and just, and will forgive our sins and cleanse us from all unrighteousness" (1 John 1:8-9).

This is all part of what I want to talk to you about— how to live with the kind of child of God you are, as your self. You certainly are special. You have been resurrected to new life in Jesus Christ, but you have not been transformed. You live still with your old nature. You are your old nature just as you are your new nature. What I want you to know is that God knows that, too. So, if you sin badly—or sin good!—or even slip sadly from what had been your hope, know that God is not shocked. God does not turn away. God expects it. Not that God *wants* you to. God simply knows it is bound to happen while we are growing up in our born-anew state. God realizes that we are beginning to exercise the muscles that are our power to live as the children of God. When we fall short, God doesn't disown us. He is indeed faithful to his promises and just in his follow-through. Remember his Word that the blood of Jesus Christ cleanses us from all sin. *That's* how we are without sin.

What I want to tell you is, "Remember that!" Not just now, but all the time. That's how to be, more and more to be, your *self*—the child of God. Remember that you've been *raised* to be God's child. It's a miracle!

Which reminds me—all of this began because I wanted to tell you the rest of the story about the daughter of Jairus.

WHAT HAPPENED NEXT?

She was raised from the dead, and Peter, James, and I were there. We were special but not-so-special, and that's the mix-up of your selves, too. The rest of the story might help you get along with your self.

Why Jesus only took the three of us along to the house of Jairus when the message came that the little girl had died, I'm not sure.

I'm sure it helped Peter later on when he was all alone with Tabitha, who had died, remember? Her Greek name was Dorcas, which means "a little deer"—and that's the pet name the synagogue president had for his little girl, too. So Peter knew what to do when they sent for him and brought him to where the woman was laid out. He said, "Tabitha, get up." And she did.

For James? Maybe the longer and the more intimately you know that God can raise the dead, the easier it is when King Herod sends the headsman to call for you, the easier it is for all of us on the way to our deaths.

For me, I think, it was so that I would start thinking this way about how to get along with that "child," your not-so-perfect self. I made the connection the second time Jesus gave Jairus's daughter a helping hand.

She was really down that day. We saw her still wiping her eyes, watching her little sister in the play yard. The Lord was good with children. You know about his taking little children in his lap and blessing them. But you don't know much about how he got along with teenagers. He didn't seem to relate very much to Dorcas that first time when he came to Jairus's house. Of course, he did take her by the hand and say to her, "Little girl, I tell you, arise!" No one else ever related that effectively! But he didn't try to talk her language or involve her in conversation at all. He did tell them to give her something to eat—which says something about how he understood teens. She was still a 12-year-old, but "going on 13" was what she told him later.

The Daughter of Jairus Raised Again

After that Jesus just slipped out. You can imagine what it was like. Little Dorcas got up and started walking, and when she opened the door and stood there, all the crying and wailing stopped and people just stared. Then the complete opposite—shouting and cheering and more crying, but for joy.

Jesus moved quickly away. When Jairus and his wife tried to thank him and urged him to stay, he only told them not to talk about it, and all of us left.

It was several weeks later—the time I began to tell you about. It just happened that the three of us were with Jesus again at the time, sitting at the edge of the play yard watching the children. Dorcas must have seen Jesus at the same time we noticed her, drying her eyes and still catching her breath in a sob the way one does after a hard cry.

She came over to Jesus, a bit shy. "I don't know if you remember me. I'm Dorcas."

"Of course, you're the daughter of Jairus." And he took her by the hand and drew her closer. "Come, sit for a while. We've held hands once before. What's been happening to you?"

At first hesitantly, but then all in a rush, it came out. She had been planning for days to go off with friends her own age that morning, and just as she was all ready with her lunch packed and sweater over her arm, set to go, her mother shouted into the house from out front, "Dorcas, you'll have to watch your sister this morning. I'm sorry about your plans, but it's Joseph's mother. She's very ill again. I must go over and help."

And then, as Dorcas began to tell what happened, the tears began again, and through her handkerchief she confessed, "I screamed and yelled and said I wouldn't and slammed the door and cried, 'Why does it always have to be me?' I was awful! And I flung myself down on my bed—you know my bed, Jesus, where I was lying when you took my hand, in that very room—and suddenly it was very quiet in the hall. There was a knock, and I heard the door open and my mother quietly said, 'Dorcas, how could you? And just after you've been raised from the dead!' I felt just awful! And I still do. How could I, Jesus? What's wrong with me? Maybe my dying didn't all go away."

Then she said, "It's not that I don't want to do what I should. I want to do good, but the good I want to do I don't do. It's the bad things I don't want to do that I do. Jesus, what's wrong with me? I'm bad, I think. Didn't I stop my dying when you raised me up?"

It was strange, Paul wrote almost the same words later on, and here was a 12-year-old little girl who had just as clear an insight on our problem as he.

Then Jesus began to explain what I've been trying to repeat to you. It wasn't only *what,* but *how* he said it, of course. "When I raised you from the dead," Jesus said, "I raised Dorcas, not some new person. You are still your self."

And when the Spirit raised *you* from the dead in Holy Baptism, it was your self that *was,* as well as your newborn nature, that had water on its head. The miracle is that you want the good and regret the bad. And that's what God-in-Jesus did for you: he raised the new you in you. That's why Paul, after he cried, "Who will deliver me from this body of death?" just gave a big cheer: "Thanks be to God through Jesus Christ our Lord!" (Rom. 7:24-25).

Jesus' face wore a half smile as he took Dorcas's little face between his hands. And he said, "Dorcas, little deer, when I raise people from the dead, I raise them *good!* It's a little bit of *my* life you have in you now. They said I shouldn't bother to come, because you were dead, but I kept coming. And that's when the miracle happened. So don't get discouraged because you feel dead again. Only believe! I keep coming. My new life keeps living in you—and it keeps coming. And the miracle happens again, when you're sorry and when you wipe your eyes and stick out your chin and decide you're going to live the new life again.

The Daughter of Jairus Raised Again

That's what you're doing right now. And it looks like your little sister fell down."

That's the way he sent her off. It's our wanting to do good, to be good, that is the wonder. "How could you?" should be asked about the good that we would, the good we want to do. And the answer to that "How could you?" is "Because you have been raised from the dead!"

"Remember that," he told her. "Remember how I took you by the hand and said, 'Arise!' "

She'll never forget that. It must be something to experience a resurrection from the dead. Even as I say that, I feel a blush rising. I thought something like that as I saw Dorcas running off to get her sister: "She's really got something to remember—a resurrection!"

And what do we have to remember? A resurrection! Ours, for one thing, but also our Lord's. The Lord is risen indeed! And we, too! We can live with our self even though it disappoints us, even though we die to our good resolves again and again. The miracle is our resurrection, and that goes on and on. We are raised again and again to new life. We live, and yet not we, but Christ lives in us.

Well, I remember two other things. One was when I was standing with Mary, Jesus' mother, on Golgatha as Jesus was dying on the cross. There were some teenagers there, too. Some were jeering along with the crowd. I haven't told before about this, but I saw Dorcas there too, eyes streaming with tears again.

And I saw her once more—in the Upper Room, a week and three days later, just after Jesus had said to Thomas, "Reach out your hand." Thomas didn't. He just fell on his knees and cried, "My Lord and my God!" But Dorcas did. She wasn't crying then, but still her eyes were full of tears. She reached out her hand and she took the hand of the Lord and she said, "Now we're both raised!"

*the Word in sacrament
remembrance*

NEXT BEST TO JESUS

The Lord's Supper Accounts

Matthew 26:26-28
Mark 14:22-24
Luke 22:14-20
1 Corinthians 11:23-25

Helps for Hearing

"Do this for the remembrance of me" was the instruction of Jesus as he first gave a piece of bread to each of his disciples to eat and said, "This is my body given for you." "Do this for the remembrance of me," he said as he gave them a cup of wine to share with the words, "This is my blood of the new covenant, shed for you for the forgiveness of sins."

It was on the night in which he was betrayed that he did this. We remember that night, but with little emphasis at all on the betrayal. What Judas did was done once and is past. Our remembering of our Lord, however, is quite a different thing. What the Lord Jesus did was done once, but it was done for *all*. The Lord's work is forever contemporary. It continually avails for all who are living. Whoever believed in Jesus the Savior in the first century, whoever believed in the middle centuries, whoever believes today, God's "so-loving-the-world" gives to them everlasting life.

WHAT HAPPENED NEXT?

The instruction to "do this for the remembrance of me," however, referred to the eating and drinking of this sacrament. Does doing that simply help us remember something done in the past? Is our doing this a memorial, something like setting aside a day to remember the end of a war to end all wars? Or does our eating and drinking make something happen, something more go on?

Much more. This sacrament, too, is continually contemporary. That has been the conviction of the church through the centuries; that is the faith of Christians today.

What is the explanation of this "by faith" conviction? What is there about the reception of bread/body, wine/blood that can effect change in us? What do we do "for the remembrance of him" that is different from simply "remembering" in the sense simply of recalling, of recollection?

One way to consider the sacrament's significance is in connection with "the Word of God." "The Word" is the term that in the Old Testament is used to describe God-at-work. God speaks God's Word, or the Word of the Lord comes, and what God wants done is done. When the Son of God came in our human nature, it is the Word that was made flesh and dwelt among us. All that Jesus accomplished in his living and dying and rising is the Word of God accomplishing what God wills. And the Word in the mouths of the disciples and of Christians since has been the source of faith in Jesus as the Savior of the world.

We believe that Word is also connected by God to water, and, used in Baptism, it also creates faith. And we believe that the Word of God, which was made flesh in Jesus Christ, is conveyed to us in the reception of the promised body and blood of the sacrament. It was by living out his perfectly obedient life in that body and by shedding his blood in a death that was a sacrifice for sinful people that Jesus saved the world. That same saving power is conveyed to us as we eat and drink his body and blood.

Next Best to Jesus

Admittedly, this sacrament is a unique, a one-of-a-kind action. But the incarnation of the Son of God and his birth and life and sacrificial death are equally so. That was done for the forgiveness of sin. This eating and drinking keeps being done, and gives us in a new way the saving means God used for that forgiveness. What our Lord did, he did once, and did for all, and needs no repetition. What we need—all that is summed up in forgiveness, namely new life and salvation—we need repeatedly. On the night he was betrayed our Lord knew that sadly enough, so he gave us this body and blood to receive "often" for renewal after betrayal.

Body, blood, eat, drink—all these terms are completely graphic and realistic. It might seem more reasonable for us to think that in this sacrament Jesus gives us *himself,* makes his whole being present to us, for us. That can be a helpful way of expressing the mystery. But his promise to "be with us always, to the close of the age" is a different presence, although it is the same risen Lord. In the sacrament he gives himself to us by this very natural process of eating and drinking, and here—his idea, not ours—he gives us the body and blood involved in gaining our salvation to sustain us in living as the saved. The Word was made body and blood and remains with us. To those who receive that body and blood he gives power to become the children of God.

What about "remembrance"? Not all the accounts of the institution of the sacrament agree in citing the words Jesus used. Translations of the words in the various accounts also vary. One modern version translates "in my memory." Many are familiar with the translation "in remembrance of me." Our rite now uses "for the remembrance of me." The words appear first of all in St. Paul's account. They are not in Mark and Matthew. Luke includes them. An imaginary account of how "do this for my remembrance" came into the rite is part of "the rest of the story." Jesus might well have used those words the first time. This might be a way to think of their significance.

Usually the Word reaches us in words; faith comes by hearing. What we hear is made meaningful in the mind. It becomes operational through the will. When we *do* this sacrament for the remembrance of our Lord's saving work, we do remember the events of his life and of his death. Words are involved in the rite. Alongside words are these sacramental elements—his body and blood. They do bring to the mind through senses other than hearing most graphically all that our Lord has achieved for us. They move us to reflection. And all of our recollecting and reflecting achieves a kind of self-proclamation. We proclaim the entire good news, mentally, to ourselves. And that achieves anew in each believer the realization of the power of God unto salvation, the personal appropriation of the power of God for our renewal in faith and life.

The mystery remains, and remains beyond us, of how the Lord gives us his body and blood, and how the benefit they gave us in his living and dying is also ours in our eating and drinking. But that they do bring us all this blessing, faith grasps; and in obedience faith does what the Lord directs in his "this do"; and in thanksgiving faith experiences all that is included in "remembrance."

And all of that is in the rest of the story.

The Rest of the Story

You can understand why I preferred the name Thaddaeus. To call me "Judas, son of James," as Luke does in his list of the Twelve, was always so cumbersome. And the name "Judas"—well, we avoid remembering Judas Iscariot. You probably think you understand why. I'm not sure if you quite do. It wasn't because we were bitter about his betraying the Lord, or that business about the financial accounts. No, it was because it was all so sad! Mostly, we all liked Judas. Jesus surely did. And we couldn't judge Judas. We all knew we each had sins enough of our own that needed forgiving.

That's not quite the way to say it. The sins were—all our sins are—forgiven. What we needed was assurance enough that the "sins enough" *were* forgiven enough! It was some added attention *we* always needed, not that our sins needed.

The Lord's Supper—that is the added assurance that we are in a state of forgiven-ness. That's what I'd really like to talk to you about. I'd like to make sure you are understanding the benefits of the Supper's eating and drinking. That night in which Jesus was betrayed, when he first said, "Take eat, this is my body" and "Take drink, this is my blood," we didn't comprehend. We could hardly be expected to. The dying and the rising hadn't happened yet. Oh, granted, if we had asked the right questions when he told us—yes, I know, told us three times how he was to be crucified and the third day rise again—then we might have understood. In any case, that's when Judas left, not understanding. Then all hell broke loose, and the power of darkness. All that happened to Jesus went on inevitably, right on to his death. And to Judas, too, to his death.

We'd like to forget how he died. The Lord's death—that's the one death that's good for remembering. I would rather say "for remembrance." "Remembering," it seems to me, suggests just recalling a past event, something which happened and is over. For me, the word *remembrance* can help us to realize that what happened is still going on, even that the best is yet to be. *Remembrance* can suggest not only bringing something to mind that did happen in the past and so, of course, isn't the same now, but can add the realization that it is nevertheless still happening in the present.

We muddle about with terms like this because we are creatures bound by time. God is always in the now. We need words to help us understand how God's now connects with our sense of time. Jesus promised that he and the Father would live *in* us, and he promised he would be *with* us always—and still we long for the conviction that he is supporting us now, that under us are the everlasting arms. *Remembrance* seems to be and is the term that can help to bring all this meaning across.

This is how *remembrance* begins in a very special way through the Lord's gift of his body and his blood. We eat and drink "for the remembrance" of all that he did and does for us. Some use the words, "in, with, and under," to describe how the Lord comes to us in the bread and wine. That's the best way I can understand what the Lord does for us in this sacrament—he gives us himself, as we knew him then, to be in, with, and under us in our now. And he does that by giving the body that lived for us and the blood that was shed for us in, with, and under the bread we eat and the wine we drink. We feel too much as if we are *now,* and all that the Lord did was *then.* We can only recall it. But the Lord's Supper makes it clear all he did goes on and on, now, that *he* goes on and on with us now. *Remembrance* brings it all together for us—as it was, as it ever shall be, is *now.*

Let me try to say it another way. Jesus is called the Word. When the Word was made flesh, Jesus was born and was with us, plain to see. We could see the glory of the Son of God. That made our minds work, and we knew the fullness of God's grace and truth. All who believed what they saw received power to become the children of God.

After his resurrection, Jesus was with us in a different way. People came to faith by hearing the Word. Thomas got in just under the wire; he was blessed both in the seeing and the hearing. So did the many others who were with us in the 40 days before Jesus' ascending out of our sight. But "blessed are those who have not seen and yet believe" (John 20:29). People heard our testimony. We were all witnesses. Our words put the Word into their minds through hearing. Faith came to them by the Word in the hearing. They received power to become the children of God. And, of course, that is still going on.

Next Best to Jesus

For all of us who still need to have that power, Jesus added another way. It is not all that unique. The first way for the Word to reach us was by sight. The second, by hearing. And this way is by eating and drinking. But, of course, this too is to bring the Word to us—and that is what "for the remembrance of me" means. It is so important for us to realize that God Almighty is in, with, and under us, that Jesus added this extra way for us to realize it, even to experience it. In this sacrament God gives us in a new way the very Word in flesh and blood that once was seen; fills our minds by this new means with the same good-news blessing which once was received only by hearing. Now each one of us is involved. We receive the body of Christ in, with, and under the bread. We receive the blood of Christ in, with, and under the wine. And—now it is for us to do it—we enter into that remembrance of him. All that God-in-Christ did for us *then* is brought into our present *now,* as we do this "for the remembrance of him." And all who believe receive new power to become more and more the children of God.

You probably still wonder how he did it in the first place. How he can do it in the thousands of places after that can be answered only by saying "with God all things are possible." But to say how Jesus did it the first time, that's possible—not how he "made it *happen,*" but how he did it.

You know that all Jewish meals begin with formal blessings. A group like ours, gathered around a rabbi as teacher, regularly had meals together that were sort of religious discussion-sessions. *That* night too began in the usual way. We were in the Upper Room each with a glass of wine over which each had said a quiet blessing to God, talking casually. We had relishes to nibble on. Then, when everything was ready and it was time to begin, we all moved to our places around the table. Jesus, as the host, began the formal blessing.

WHAT HAPPENED NEXT?

He took a small loaf of bread from the table and began the prayer we always pray: "Blessed be Thou, O Lord our God, eternal King, who bringest forth bread from the earth...." After the prayer, it was always the practice for the host to take a bit of the loaf and then to pass the loaf to the first in the circle. That person took a piece and passed the loaf, and so on. It was always a very quiet few minutes. But *that* night in the silence, as the bread went from hand to hand, we heard Jesus say, "Take and eat. This is my body which is given for you."

Well, you can imagine! We looked at one another with raised eyebrows, turned heads. No one understood what he could mean. Now we do—better, at least. But that was the first time.

Then the meal went on, and during it our discussion always began. *That* night it was mostly Jesus who talked. Much of it was praying, praying out loud, asking the Father to glorify him, that the time had come, and praying for us. You know that high priestly prayer. He prayed for all of you too. He prayed for all who would come to faith through our word. And you have—right?—after generations of witnesses.

But back to how the supper began. Now the meal and the talking were over. Always the last thing—we called it "the cup of blessing"—went like this. Jesus took a cup of wine and prayed a long formal prayer thanking God for the covenant God had made with Israel. He took a sip of the wine and passed it around the circle, just as the bread had been passed. In the hush each one took a sip. But that night we heard him say, "Take and drink, all of you. This cup is the new covenant in my blood which is shed for you and for many for the forgiveness of sin."

Again—you can imagine! His blood, and "all of you, drink." We'd been used to blood being shed in the Temple sacrifices. But we'd too often thought of sacrifice as something we gave to God as sort of a payment; we thought of the blood being offered to God to appease God. *This* meant *we* were the ones who needed the sacrifice for sin in our very selves. And, of course, this, he said, was *his* blood, and said that it set up a new covenant, which meant the old covenant was over. After these years, though, I think the most significant thing was that the Lord did not make a point of saying "which *will* be shed" as if he were referring just to the coming cross and his shedding of his blood. What he would be doing for us would always be going on and on in everyone's now, and that "once for all" shedding of his blood would be shared through all the years by those who celebrated this supper "in remembrance of him."

Then we sang the hymn and left for the garden.

That's how he did it.

Now I can tell you what *I* did. It is my contribution to all of you who have been celebrating the supper ever since. It was the first Lord's Day, the evening. The doors of the Upper Room were locked in fear, but inside, the mood was perhaps best described as amazed—but like a victory celebration. Everyone was saying to everyone else, "The Lord is risen!" And everyone was replying, "He is risen indeed!" Mary Magdalene had to tell her story over and over, and the two from Emmaus, and Peter. Gradually there were no more questions, was no more discussion. For me it is another example of the difference between "remembering" and "remembrance." There had been all this "remembering" of what *had* happened, and now there was this intense joy at knowing it was *still* happening. Jesus is still doing what he told us he came to do. God is *still* doing all that God *did* do. "Remembering" the last days changed to "remembrance," and the sudden, relaxed, expectant quiet seemed to say everyone knew it.

Peter and I were standing by the table on which people had placed the food and drink they had brought for a common meal. In the quiet Peter picked up a loaf, looked at all of us, looked at me, and I said quietly, "As often as you do it . . . !"

WHAT HAPPENED NEXT?

Peter nodded and said, "It *is* time for a celebration." And he began the prayer of blessing over the bread. Then he broke off a piece for himself and passed the loaf along. It took longer. There were more than just 12. The quiet was as if time had stopped. In the hush—I couldn't hold back—I said, so softly perhaps only Peter heard, I said, "Say it, Peter. Say what he said. Say the words he said, in remembrance of him!"

Peter looked at me, wondering, and then he took up the words and said quietly—but all could hear—"That night our Lord said, 'Take and eat. This is my body given for you.'" Then he looked straight at me and added, "We do this in remembrance of him."

Just then it happened—Jesus appeared! And he said, "Peace be unto you!" Talk about the real presence!

You know all that happened then, and we all knew. We all said, "It is the Lord!"

Finally the potluck. Jesus didn't stay for that, though he did eat a bit of fish. I still have this vivid sense that when he disappeared, no one felt that he had left at all. No one said something silly like, "He's gone again." All those moments were filled with completeness, like, "It is finished." Nothing had been said about how we had all fled or about our doubt and despair—and some of us had really been angry at Jesus for how he had disappointed us. No, it was all done. Forgiveness *was*. Forgiveness *is*. All he said was that we should forgive, and whosoever's sins we would forgive, they were forgiven. He was alive. Life *is*. We all felt it. What was going on was "remembrance."

After we had eaten, we were milling about, and spontaneously we all began to do what later we called "passing the peace." We would greet a person by name and say, "The peace of the Lord be with you." Now to tell you this last story I have to say that I come from Nazareth, just like Nathaniel. It was Nathaniel, you remember, to whom Philip came saying, "We have found the Messiah. It is Jesus from

Next Best to Jesus

Nazareth." And Nathaniel said, "Can any good thing come out of Nazareth?" Often Philip would not use my name Thaddaeus—not when Nathaniel was within earshot. He would refer to me as "the second-best thing to come out of Nazareth." But that night Philip met me to share the peace and said, "Thaddaeus, the peace of the Lord be with you." Then he gently punched me on the arm with his fist and added, "You second-best thing to come out of Nazareth."

I was about to reply, but Peter's voice rose above the sound of voices. He was ready to pray the prayer over the cup of blessing, the thanks to God for the covenant. He took a sip from the cup, passed it to the next, and so on—and in the quiet he said, "Take and drink. This cup is the new covenant in his blood which is shed for you for the forgiveness of sin." He looked at me again and added, "We do this for the remembrance of him."

And we did. When the benediction was said, and I could say what I'd started to say to Philip, I gestured with both hands at all the company and included all we had done, and I said, "No, Philip, *this* is the next-best thing to come out of Nazareth."

assurance
subjective justification

70 x 7—490 AND COUNTING

The Unmerciful Servant and The Merciful Savior

Matthew 18:21-35

Helps for Hearing

Would God expect us to do something God wouldn't do?

The Lord makes very clear what God expects. God-in-Christ counted out 70 times 7 as the number of times we should be ready to forgive those who sin against us. Does it work the other way? Can we confidently expect 490 forgivenesses from God?

A more urgent question: where are we statistically? Can you estimate the number of times you have sinned against God? And even if you have been a slow starter, what about sin number 491?

Finally, the question which brings the whole problem down to where we live, where each one of us lives—alone: Does God forgive *me*? Conceivably, in order to salvage something out of this created world, God might declare a general amnesty and forgive the entire world. But even then, how about *me,* me personally? Not necessarily because I am "chief of sinners"—that may even be part of my uncertainty. Will God forgive my not feeling particularly a major sinner at all? How can I, day after day—and sometimes hourly—make myself the subject of the sentence: "*I* am forgiven!" In the church's teaching that is what is called "subjective justification." Am I the specific subject of God's love and forgiveness?

Phrased in a doctrine called "objective justification," theology asserts that God-in-Christ has forgiven *the world,* and whoever believes that, *has* everlasting life. But has God done that for me, a Johnny-come-lately? Is it all *for me*? Can I have the confidence to be the subject of the Christian assertion, "I am forgiven!" Blessed assurance!

Jesus' story of the unmerciful servant follows immediately after the 70 x 7 answer to Peter. The Hebrew legalist's usual formula was to forgive three times. Peter went for seven. The multiplicant 490 must have left him stunned. Admittedly, just among us brothers and sisters, it would be unique circumstances that would see us sticking around the sibling who would persist in offending us 490 times. After all one's cheeks had been turned, one would take off. But God is with us always. Poor *us* God has always with him. It is the same God over and over again with whom we have to do. Will God stick with us?

It is not that God is especially thin-skinned and takes offense easily. The fact is that God is a jealous God in the nature of things. God is the only one who does not sin in being jealous. That is what God must do. It is the divine right. God would be failing in God-ness if any sinning were simply tolerated. The holiness of the Trinity must seek a mirror image in those created in God's likeness. The number 491 shows up very quickly on our total bill if we follow through on Jesus' words and take an accounting.

Follow through on the account of the unmerciful servant as well. Our multiplication must handle not only sins

70 x 7—490 and Counting

directly against God as the party of the first part, but also sins against the second table of the law and the parties of the second part, our neighbors. When the sum of all we do and do not do over against them is fairly faced, the next sound we hear is the clang of the prison door. The point of the story is that we should forgive others as we are forgiven by God. But the rest of the story is, "What if we do not?" Are we not in debtor's prison until we have paid "the uttermost farthing"?

Or until someone else does! A theory of the atonement that tries to explain with "debts" and "payments" how God's justifying of sinners is worked out does not compute well. The figure of God is strained when pictured as demanding payment. The biblical phrase, "... to the third and fourth generation" has a fierce sound, but is more vague than selling the servant into slavery *with* his spouse and children. And the good news—could a good God take the balance of payments *we* owe out of the saving account of the Son—no, even more, out of his skin? But when 490 equates with a cell and the key thrown away, we—all of us—are desperate to subscribe to the theory of the vicarious atonement: that our debts are covered by the payment of the life and death of the Son of God. It covers us even when we have reached a debt of 490 and are still counting.

Another way to say it is that we believe Good Friday.

The disciples did not understand the predictions Jesus gave of his death, of the details of mocking and spitting and whipping and crucifying, and they were afraid to ask questions. It was after the fact that the church asked how it all worked. How could sinners' barbarous crucifying of the holy and just one make possible God's eternal forgiveness? Yes, the wages of sin is death. The dying of a sinless one could be explained as somehow making credit available so that sinners would not have to pay up themselves. Or, alternately, the offering to the Father God of the perfect obedience of God the Son substituted for our consistent disobedience.

WHAT HAPPENED NEXT?

No explanation seems adequate. But start counting to 490 and beyond. Look about you at the walls of the debtor's prison to which we are sentenced for life and death. What we need, what we want, is for Jesus to take our place here in this debtor's prison so that we can get out. We *must* cry out to God for something like the vicarious, substitutionary, atoning death of Jesus Christ—and his resurrection.

Put them together, then, the good God and that Friday and that Sunday. No wonder then that we call the Friday *good* and see Easter as even better.

But what about when Friday and Sunday do not seem to take care of Monday through Thursday, and Saturday, too, is dubious?

The answer is "Listen to the pardon again"—and again and again. The Word is "You are forgiven!" When you are so despondent some days that you dare not even rattle the bars of your cage, hear the good news and push at them. The door swings free. Thank God, it's Friday every day of the week.

You who have hesitatingly or joyfully experienced the door of debtor's prison swinging open, but who on some days feel you must get properly dressed and look respectable before you can walk out where others can see you, hear the cry of Good Friday: "Get out of here! Just as you are, with just that one plea, 'He died for me!'"

You who have come out of prison, accepting the Lord's repayment, thankful for the balanced books, but who have sinned again, you—even with a sort of perverse pride in being so responsible for your own wrongdoing, crawling down the dungeon steps again and putting your wrists in chains again and lying down and suffering again—don't do it! Hear Easter's cry, "Free at last!" And with the Lord, rise up!

Good Friday and Easter mean a love so great you never even have to say you're sorry. God knows you are, and—God knows—you are forgiven!

70 x 7—490 and Counting

The Rest of the Story

Perhaps the dreams began because Jesus multiplied an adequate 7 by an impossible 70.

"If a brother keeps sinning against me," the question had begun, "how often should I forgive? Seven times?"

And then came the multiplication. Jesus said, "Not only until 7 times, but until 70 times 7."

Perhaps the dreams began because Jesus added the story about the unmerciful servant right after his multiplication. The point was immediately clear. The story described the way people were not expected to act if they were really God's people, members of the kingdom of God. A servant who owed the king millions was forgiven because the king felt sorry for him. But that servant turned right around and demanded payment of a debt amounting to a few dollars owed him by a fellow servant. When the king heard about it, he was very angry.

No doubt the Lord's point was that we should forgive as God has forgiven us. There is a parallel to that point which is difficult to ignore—that God will be very angry if kingdom people do not forgive as God has forgiven us. But who can forgive as God forgives? Perhaps the dreams began because of that.

The punishments were so crushing! The king ordered that the debtor servant should be sold as a slave, together with his wife and children and all that he had. And then the punishment the servant brought down on his fellow debtor—that he should be thrown into jail until he should pay the debt. Debtor's prison—the ultimate catch–22 situation. Could all that be heard simply as local color to give the story impact? Perhaps the dreams began because of that.

The dreams probably began because the king was clearly God, and when God hears that his people do not forgive as God forgives—and the formula is 70 times 7—then God will condemn those servants to prison and torture until everything is paid. That clearly means forever. Jesus made it explicit: "That is how my Father in heaven will treat every one of you unless you forgive from your heart." The dreams began because of that.

The dreams did not merely repeat the circumstances of the story. A few at the beginning were about being ready to forgive. There was the night Peter was so furious with James and John. He had heard how they had tried to get the guarantee of seats on the right and left hand when Jesus sat on his throne as king. The presumption! And Peter knew he didn't want to forgive, not one bit. That night in the dream he was the unforgiving servant thrown into debtor's prison.

But then the dreams began to change. They began to include all different kinds of sins. The dreams seemed to have made the logical deduction that if God would act so furiously over our not forgiving, the punishment would be equally awful for our not fulfilling the other commands of God. After the time—three times—when he had said, "I know not the man," after the cursing and swearing, the dream was terrible. And after that, any little thing could trigger the dream, because it was clear there *were* no little things wrong. Every wrong thing was a big sin.

But it was mostly the accumulation of minor things that he dreamed of. In the dream he was always in debtor's prison, sometimes for things very recent, but sometimes for things done even in childhood.

The ten cents kept back from the change when he had been sent to the grocery at the last minute to get a forgotten something for supper.

The time he was terribly flip with his mother when she had confronted him with some sloppy habit he had picked up, and he had brushed her aside with an airy, "Well, you'll just have to get used to it." It wasn't that he hadn't paid for that, and it wasn't unresolved; his mother had hugged him after it was all over, but it was that he still felt guilty about it. Foolish, too, of course.

Then the much more serious things—well, who decides what's serious about sins?—but the angry recriminations against his wife, the times he flew off the handle so suddenly, so fiercely, against his daughter.

There were some things only God knew about, but that he remembered clearly, and they were things God explicitly cared about and had made up commandments against and carved them in stone and had them translated into English and had him memorize them in confirmation instruction class, and he could recite them to this day.

What was worse than all the main commandments were all those things added to the "what does this mean" after the commandments. Those were the things that got you coming and going, things like "defend them, speak well of them, and put the best construction on everything," and "help and befriend them in every bodily need" and explanations of coveting that left everything so vague—"not wanting anything you weren't supposed to want, or wanting it too much."

He had reason enough to feel guilty about a lot of those things because they seemed to repeat themselves in spite of all the tears, the remorse, the resolving, the repenting he had done. There was always so much you ought to do. Everywhere you looked there were people holding out their hands. They followed you all the way to the bank, and just as that preacher had said, "If you look closely, you can see in their hungry hands the mark of the nails." And social justice and political action. It's true he defended peoples' right to their opinion even though he didn't agree with them or with some of the ways they went about putting their point across; but the fact is that he didn't *do* anything about any of the issues, and felt guilty about it.

(It's no use saying "he" any more. Let's admit it and say "we.")

The strange thing sometimes about the jail in the dream is that we seem to have built it ourselves, for ourselves. We don't *have* to go to jail, but we seem determined to go anyway, to put ourselves in—and we feel guilty about that. We stumble down the worn granite steps on our own, without any jailer forcing us. We sit down on the straw, which is quite dry and comfortable, and even from the floor we can see out the window where the blue sky and the light are close by. So it's not very realistic, and things are not very dungeon-like, and we feel a little guilty about that. We have to work at feeling bad, and we feel guilty about that.

But the most terrible thing about the dream is when we've convinced ourselves that God has started counting. If we are to forgive as God forgives, then the 490 times that Jesus recommended for our forgiving is the total forgivings to be expected from God. If divine mercy's total is 490, how far along is God with the count against us? We begin to audit our books and count our sins we can remember. We know we can't remember them all and know that God does, and so we round them off to tens. But we keep feeling we must examine ourselves and draw the bottom line. And we do, and soon we are up to 488 and then easily remember number 489 and then number 490. We've reached 70 times 7 and still counting.

What to do? Can we be resolved what to do on Good Friday?

Push the dream past fiction and fantasy into fact, into God's truth.

In the flesh or out of the flesh, it matters not. When you have counted to the limit of 490, be caught up, past guards and prison gates, and look for Jesus Christ.

Find him on the Way of Sorrows. We'll know how to recognize him, the man carrying the rough cross, his back scourged; the man with the crown of thorns on his head, his brow bleeding. We fall on our knees there on the cobblestones of the roadway, bringing the whole procession to a stop-action halt. We know what to say: "I have sinned against heaven and against thee, and now it is 491! Lord,

70 x 7—490 and Counting

have mercy!" And the Lord rests the base of his cross for a moment on the road, looks at us with a half smile of sympathy, with a finger brushes sweat and blood from above one eyebrow and then from the other, and says gently, "Did you understand me to say until 490 times? I meant forever and ever!" And he takes a deep breath, shoulders the cross, and as suddenly as it stopped the whole procession moves into action again. And we see Simon the Cyrenian stepping off the curb and coming across the street.

If the counting goes on, or if it begins again, if you do again what you have many times promised was done for the last time, and the total goes up to 492, look for the Lord again. By now he has reached Golgotha. The horrible nailing is done, and the Son of Man is lifted up. And he draws us to him along with the two drawn sinners on the right hand and the left. Fall before him and say, "My Lord, my King, I have sinned against your Father and against my Father, against your God and my God, and against you—and now it is 492! Lord, have mercy!"

See the Lord tense his muscles and shift his weight, as if the body burden on the foot piece and the nails has become even heavier. Then he says to us, "Did you understand me to say until 490 times? I meant forever and ever!"

Then time's passing begins again, his head turning toward Dismas, he says, "Today—paradise!"

If the counting goes on, or if you have dug up again something you buried and dug up and buried again and again, if this time it is as vivid and flagrant and as bitterly regretted as when first you committed it, but if this time you have counted it and it is numbered, and its number is 493, look for the Lord again. He has not come down from the cross. He gives a loud cry, and time pauses—as if waiting for us, for our tears and our confession.

"Remember, O Lord, back there, back then. I have gone over it with you time and again. Remember my tears. I do remember the absolution, those words Sunday after Sunday.

WHAT HAPPENED NEXT?

But it haunts me still. I have counted again and it is 493! Lord, have mercy!" The dying Lord says, "Did you understand me to say until 70 x 7? I meant forever and ever!" And we hear the echo of his cry, "It is finished!"

When you see him again, as see him you shall, after Good Friday, after your good Fridays, after your counting, when you see him again, as see him you shall, after the three days, after he is risen indeed, it will be forever and ever!

faith and hope
the resurrection

EASTER WITHOUT SPICES

The Women and the Empty Tomb

Mark 16:1-8

Helps for Hearing

If Christ did not rise from the dead, we can have no eternal hope, not for our own resurrection nor for this life. If Christ be not raised, we are of all people the most miserable. But now *is* Christ raised and become the first fruits of them that slept. From faith in the resurrection comes hope.

How is faith given? That seems a better way to ask it than, "How do I get faith?" It is a gift. No one can say the things we say about Jesus Christ but by the Holy Spirit's gift of faith. We say that he is the Lord of heaven and earth, that he is the Son of God, the Word made flesh, that his death was a sacrifice removing the death sentence from the whole sinning world, that he has risen from the dead and that there is a resurrection to life eternal for all who believe in him. Only by the Spirit of God who gives the insight, the faith, can one accept as true these unbelievable things, can one stake all true existence in this life and all hope for a life after death on these incredible facts.

Here, perhaps, more than in any other aspect of the work of the Holy Spirit the passage applies, "The wind blows where it wills" (John 3:8). It would seem obvious that one would have to *know* about these things before one could believe them. But not everyone who knows all these things has faith. It would seem obvious that "faith comes from what is heard, and what is heard comes by the preaching of Christ" (Rom. 10:17). One must hear about the risen Lord to believe. But many have heard about the resurrection and still have no faith through that hearing. It is by the Word of God that hearing is made effective and faith is given. That is only another way of saying that it is by God doing God's work in God's own way that faith can be created by hearing. That Word must even make hearing effective if it is to be the origin of faith.

Three times before it all happened Jesus told his disciples that he would be put to death. Three times he told them *how* he would be put to death. Three times he clearly said that on the third day after his death he would be raised from the dead. But when the dying happened just as he had said, they believed he was dead, because they saw it, but they did not believe he would return to life because he had said it. They accepted what they saw, that he was indeed dead; but even that was not faith that his death would give them life. They seemed to have learned nothing from what they had heard. Certainly they did not believe from what they had heard of his death.

In the same way they did not believe, they seemed even to have learned nothing, from what they had heard about his resurrection from the dead. Nor did they believe their eyes when they saw. Thomas was very specific about not trusting what he heard, and insisted that only after seeing and touching would he believe. When he did believe, it was through the presence of Jesus himself. He had no need to touch. Faith was a gift to him, and he cried, "My Lord and my God!" There is a greater power involved in the Word than basic hearing. God must be in the hearing, even as God was at work in the flesh.

Nevertheless, it is clear that God's Word-work relies heavily on hearing: "How are they to believe in him of whom they have never heard?" (Rom. 10:14). The Word relied as well on seeing: "He presented himself alive after his passion by many proofs" (Acts 1:3). To the Word's arsenal God adds sacraments. They reach the other senses after the visibility of Christ's presence was withdrawn.

In spite of all those impacts of the Word, however, there are many who do not believe. They are not persuaded nor convinced that God was in Christ reconciling the world to himself. Deeper than that, they do not accept the gift of faith, which God would give them, that all which Jesus Christ did in his life and death was "for us and for our salvation."

The mystery of the gift remains: why do some believe and some do not? But equally basic, the task remains: the church is to tell all this good news to all the world to make disciples, believers, baptizing them in the name of the Holy Trinity. Here, clearly, we are to work as if all depends on us; but more clearly still, all depends on God.

The tremendous significance of our testimony is underscored as Jesus transfers his own being sent to the world by the Father to the disciples: "even so I send you" (John 20:21). He prayed in his last hours "for those who believe in me through their word" (John 17:20). The thousands who were moved to faith and repentance heard Peter preach the resurrection at Pentecost. Those on Mars Hill in Athens did not believe because, in part, at least, they turned Paul off and rejected as impossible the resurrection from the dead which he preached.

For us all then the resurrection of Jesus Christ is the mystery of faith. The resurrection is the creation and the foundation of our faith. It is the basis of our hope. "[Christ was] designated Son of God in power ... by his resurrection from the dead" (Rom. 1:4). We who by hearing of this Word came to faith, by the same Word heard are sustained and strengthened in that faith. Yet, even as our Lord's words to Thomas are a comfort to us ("Blessed are those who have not seen and yet believe"), we rejoice as well in the gift of the Word that we can in a sense see—in bread and wine and in water. We, like the women at that first Easter morning, need the Word of our Lord's resurrection to infuse meaning into all he did in life and all he achieved by his death. Very early in the morning at the rising of the sun—or at the eleven o'clock service—we come with haste to receive the Word in all its forms, as it is read or spoken or given in the body and blood. With it comes strengthening of faith, the increase of love and hope.

The ending of the Gospel according to St. Mark has been a continuing puzzle. There the direct experience of seeing the empty tomb where the body of the Lord had been placed, and even of hearing the specific announcement of his resurrection, left the women distressed and terrified. They were afraid and said nothing to anyone. That is the way the account ends. But that is completely different from the way the resurrection climax of Jesus has effected faith in the lives of millions. Other new endings to this Gospel that would more completely testify to the power of the Word in the resurrection have been handed down through the years. Mark's purpose in writing his account was evidently served by this abrupt ending, but for us the good news is the rest of the story. And part of the good news is that it is never too late to share the good news. And a greater share in the joy of that Easter—there is still time—can be a part of the rest of your story.

The Rest of the Story

It is what happened—what Mark's Gospel says. We were afraid, terribly afraid, and so we said nothing to anybody.

Easter without Spices

But we could not keep silent for long. We want to tell you, tell you now. We're glad we're not too late.

It wasn't just afterwards that we were afraid. Before we saw the empty tomb and the young man in the white robe sitting on the right side, we were frightened. All of us were frightened much before that. Even before the mob arrested him, but especially after that. Taken to Pilate's court, then Herod's, the horrible scourging and the mockery—you know all that. It's dreadful just to recall it. And the long way carrying his cross, finally the crucifixion and the hours of suffering, the darkness from noon until he died—we were watching from a distance through it all.

The three of us, Mary of Magdala, Mary the mother of James the younger and of Joseph, and I, Salome, had the idea first. Well, not really first. We remembered the woman who brought an alabaster jar of pure nard and poured the perfume on Jesus' head. There was a lot of criticism, but Jesus defended her. He said she had anointed his body ahead of time for his burial. And now it was time for his burial. It was too late for him to know it, but we wanted to do something, too, out of our love and our grief. None of us had the kind of money it would take, nor could we buy the spices, because it was nearly the Sabbath. We decided to ask some of the other women if they wanted to go in on it with us. Just thinking about it made us all break down. We were in tears when Benjamin, one of the men who worked for Nicodemus, came by.

(The voices of the women go silent, and the gruff voice of a man takes over.)

I stopped and asked what was the matter. You can't just ignore three women crying their eyes out. Actually I was on the way to the shops to buy a mixture of myrrh and aloes for Nicodemus, because *he* was going in with Joseph of Arimathea, who had Pilate's permission to take the body of Jesus from the cross. And I was in a hurry because of the Sabbath.

WHAT HAPPENED NEXT?

Well, they told me what they wanted to do, and for good measure asked me if I wanted to be part of it. Of course, I said I was already in on one plan. We had a linen cloth, and with the spices we were going to prepare his body for burial. But they said what *they* planned was to anoint his body on Sunday, after the sabbath. "A sort of memorial," they said, "because it's so awful" and "all hope is gone" and "we'll never see him again"—and then more tears.

I felt bad enough myself. Jesus was a good man. But he would certainly be dead, and one anointing with spices would surely be enough. He would be dead before sundown and even more dead in three days. What was the use? It was too late. It was all a waste. Killing him was a waste. He was no criminal. He was the best ever was—by then I was in tears too—but he's dead, I said, and there's the end of it.

But they insisted they were going to do it, to anoint his body as a token of their love, and would I buy nard for them while I was at the shop—on credit, no less. And there we were, all sort of laughing at the "on credit" bit and crying and saying things like "all we'd hoped for," and, "Why didn't God *do* something?" and, "Now it's too late." By then I was so worked up and so full of despair I agreed to buy the nard with the change from the money Nicodemus had given me. But what was the use? We had hoped he was Israel's Messiah, but what can you expect from a man who lets himself be put to death? Yes, lets himself. He saved others. He could have saved himself. He even raised others from the dead.

(A woman's voice begins to speak. Maybe you can recognize whose voice it is.)

I'm glad they asked me. But somehow I never seem to have more than two mites in my purse. My husband used to handle the money when he was alive. Of course, that's not the only reason now. I never *have* more. I can't get ahead of all it costs to keep us going at home. But I'm glad they asked me. He was so kind about the two mites in the temple collection box. One of the disciples told me later on.

Easter without Spices

And I heard him at Mary and Martha's house when Lazarus was dead. "I am the resurrection and the life," he said. "Whoever lives and believes in me shall never die" (John 11:26). And yet Lazarus had died. They thought he was too late. But Jesus brought him to life again. I just don't understand. He said that he was the resurrection and the life. And he did make Lazarus alive.

But now Jesus is dead. I believed the same as Mary did that he was the Messiah, the Son of God, who was to come into the world. We believed he had come. But that's all over now. Dying doesn't leave a person much of a Messiah. Dying doesn't seem like much of a way to save the rest of us. He's dead. But, oh, we loved him. I'm glad they asked me. Only two mites, of course. It was all I had. More this time than that other time. I wished I had more. But it was all I had for Jesus, dead Jesus, for a memorial for Jesus. I'm glad they asked me.

(Another voice takes over, saying only that her name was Anne.)

I got there too late, too late, too late. My daughter, Susannah, has been sickly ever since her father died. His was a fever too; lingered on and on. And then he died. Left just the two of us. And she started up with a fever just like her daddy. All at once I decided—I was desperate—I was going to bring her to Jesus. So I came all this way, but I was too late. I came too late! They told me he'd been arrested. So what could I do? I've managed this little room by the edge of the cemetery—one little window, but it looks out over the garden. You see some sepulchers over there, never been used.

But there's nothing I can do. Just sit here by her side and pray. I had hoped they'd let him off. He's never done anything wrong. But now they told me he's dead, and they're collecting for a memorial of ointment. They didn't ask me for anything. They know I don't have anything any more—just Susannah, my daughter. But I told them I want to go

WHAT HAPPENED NEXT?

along, early in the morning before sunrise on Sunday. Maybe my daughter's fever will have broken by then.

(The wistful voice fades away. A voice from among the three women takes up the story. It is Salome again.)

The strangest reply we got was when we asked Zebedee's wife. You have to know her to appreciate this. We asked her if she wanted to go along Sunday at sunrise and if she wanted to help with buying the nard. She snapped at us: "What foolishness! Of course I want to go along! Sunday, right, the third day. But don't waste your money on spikenard. We won't need any spices, not on the third day!"

And that's all she would say, even though we argued that the nard was the whole point of the memorial. She just said again, "Foolishness. We won't need any spices on the third day."

And that was it! That's how it turned out. We three were together carrying the nard Benjamin had brought us. Anne didn't show up. We thought she had probably overslept after sitting up with her daughter, or perhaps she couldn't leave her. But Mrs. Zebedee came, with a very "mother of the sons of thunder" look about her. She didn't say anything, not even when she saw the jar in which we were carrying the spikenard with which to anoint the body of Jesus. She waved her hand at the jar as if to say with a gesture what she had said before. And we remembered how she had said, "We won't need any spices, not on the third day." And we wondered.

Suddenly we thought about the large stone that had been rolled in front of Joseph's sepulcher. It was too late to do anything about it, so we went on. We all gasped at the same time as we saw it; the stone was rolled away. We ran and looked into the grave.

There was a youth wearing a white robe, nobody we knew, sitting on the right side of the place where the body of Jesus should have been—but wasn't! The body was not there! We were dumbfounded.

Easter without Spices

But that was only the beginning. The young man spoke, a haunting sort of voice: "Do not be amazed; you seek Jesus of Nazareth, who was crucified. He has risen, he is not here; see the place where they laid him" (Mark 16:6). And he pointed. But he needn't have. That was what was so frightening. Jesus had been dead. And now? Risen? Alive?

The young man again: "Go, tell his disciples and Peter that he is going before you to Galilee; there you will see him, as he told you" (Mark 16:7).

Well, you know the rest. We got out of there and fled from the tomb. We were beside ourselves with terror. And we said nothing to anyone. We were . . . we really were afraid! But we have to tell someone. We must. And so we are telling you. We're glad we're not too late. We're all here, I think. Where is Mrs. Zebedee? Well, no matter. She probably stopped at her house.

(Just then that other voice again—Anne, the woman whose daughter was ill. She is all smiles, but first she apologizes).

I was too late. I fully intended to go with you. I overslept. When I did wake up, I looked out the little window into the garden and saw the sun was already well up. I knew I was too late to catch you. But the most amazing thing! I saw a woman in the garden, and she was talking to a tall man—the gardener, I thought. As I watched, she fell to her knees and reached out to grasp the man, but he backed away, looking as if he were explaining something to her. Then he began to talk, and he looked up at me where I was staring at the whole scene. He smiled, waved up at me, and he said, "It's a good morning, Anne." I'd never seen him before. Then, as I said, he waved his hand in a half salute, half blessing, and I could barely hear him say, "Be of good cheer," and he disappeared. And I looked around to tell someone—and there was Susannah, my little girl, sitting up, rubbing her eyes and stretching. And the fever is gone! She's well! And I was so relieved. I tucked her in. She fell into a deep sleep. And I climbed into bed and slept too—and here it is already afternoon!

The three women looked at one another. "We can't carry on like this. We have to let the disciples know. Especially Peter."

As they talked back and forth there were sounds at the door—voices. Someone looked in and said, "We're all getting together in the Upper Room."

Other voices too: "Be careful." "Go singly." "Keep your eyes open."

"It will be all right," they said. "They'll lock the door and cover the windows. Just knock and say, 'Peace.'"

"It's potluck. Bring what you have."

We all looked at one another. And Mary said, "I've a loaf of bread that's fresh enough still." And she went to the kitchen to get it.

Just then who should come in but Mrs. Zebedee. She must have come from her house with the others on the way to the Upper Room and had stopped for us. Mrs. Zebedee said, "I've got a bottle of wine I've been saving, waiting for something really worth celebrating."

"It will be enough," someone said.

The bread and the wine were just enough.

We separated after agreeing to join one another at the stairs to the Upper Room. And when we were together we went up.

We knocked and said the password, "Peace." They let us in through the heavy door. And what a buzz! What excitement! We almost didn't get a chance to tell anyone anything, because everyone was telling us. Well, it's never too late to get in on something as big as the resurrection!

Mary Magdalene had seen him in the garden—just before Anne did, probably.

And Simon Peter kept going around saying, "The Lord is risen indeed!"

Easter without Spices

There were two disciples who had walked and talked with him on the road to Emmaus. They said they had recognized the Lord at supper when he took the bread and blessed it and began to break it.

That reminded us of the bread and the wine we had brought along. We gave it to Peter. Then he called the whole room to attention, and they gathered together around him. He began, "Remember how he said, 'Do this for my remembrance'? We have this bread. We have this wine."

The bread and the wine were just enough.

Oh, and about Mrs. Zebedee, the one who said we wouldn't need any spices, not on the third day? She didn't say anything to anybody either, and we especially appreciated that she didn't say, "I told you so."

witnessing

HE GOES WITH YOU

Matthew 16:13-25

Helps for Hearing

There is not very much "gazing up into heaven" going on in our world today, as we see the disciples doing in Acts 1. Probably there is considerably more "waiting in the city," the church waiting for more of the gifts of the Spirit. The charge to go to the uttermost parts of the earth is being obeyed more, perhaps, than the "beginning in Jerusalem." Our concern with our personal witness—"you *are* witnesses of all these things"—is always pertinent. The 40 days of having the blessing of occasional sight as well as the promise of greater blessing for those who believe without sight is a useful time to think of our witness. And that witness is *our* word, the homely word, the neighborly word. The Spirit adds the power.

All of Lent is a time of preparation. We prepare for a faithful celebration of Easter. But Easter itself is more than a day; it is a season. From Easter to Pentecost are the "Great Fifty Days." "All that Jesus began to do and to teach" was preparation for the disciples. And their task was "Go, therefore ..." We too have learned and believed and have received the assignment.

WHAT HAPPENED NEXT?

Traditional midweek Lenten services might helpfully be extended to the Wednesday of Easter week. Witnessing could be the accent of a "Great Fifty Days" service as a Pentecost climax to Lent and Eastertide.

Epiphany's accent on revelation has always challenged the church to its task of witness. The last Wednesday in Epiphany might lend itself to a final accent on a program of invitation to the Lenten midweek services throughout the community.

We are all in need of "Helps for Doing" the witness our Lord asks for us. What can we imagine the conversations were like when two disciples entered a house in a village? Did they begin with crops and weather and "Where do you come from?" Then were they able to mention the Master? And then they had to lead the villagers from curiosity about the miracles to the real message of the kingdom, the good news, and the new possibilities in the Savior.

Our normal conversations begin in much the same way. Often "the church I go to" is the intermediary subject (the miracles are less in the news today). But the final task of changing the subject to King and kingdom talk remains. And it is that gospel talk which is finally the power of God to change the subject to whom we are witnessing.

Are the lists of the 12 apostles as they are recorded in the Gospels set out in pairs? Is this pairing the way they went out, two by two? The combinations in the Gospel listings do not always agree; but Judas Iscariot is always listed last. Who goes out with Simon the Zealot? All of us feel added to the pairs. With Judas gone there will always be an odd one out. The last person called will have no one to go along. And that one alone is always—you. Doesn't our Lord see that? And doesn't he say, "And I will go with you!" For he does. Always.

In any case, and at any time, it is clear that what each one of us does and says in our witness is the rest of the story.

He Goes with You

The Rest of the Story

Yours is the rest of the story. What *we* did is recorded in the New Testament. You are the ones who are writing the Newer Testament. Ours is indeed a worthy witness of all that God has done. But your own testimony has a special strength. It is what God has done for us *lately*. The Lord prayed—the Lord prays—for those who will believe through our word. That part is being done. Our part is to say something to somebody.

Peter said to me late one evening, "I find it very difficult to urge people to give a faithful and true witness to Jesus Christ. I always seem to hear a rooster crowing."

Ask not for whom the rooster crows. It crows for you.

From what I hear, you are, if anything, a bit amazed at how bold and brash we were to go out preaching when Jesus first sent us out two by two. And you are as astounded as we were at the great outpouring of the Spirit and the thousands who believed as we witnessed after the resurrection. But sometimes I feel that you come down rather hard on us for some other things: that we all fled at the time of the arrest, that Peter denied the Lord three times, that we had no confidence during those terrible hours before the third day's rising. The focus of your criticism often seems to be our reaction—three times, too—when Jesus told us in advance how he would be crucified and the third day rise again. We didn't understand what he meant. The saying was hidden from us. We were afraid to ask any questions. Is it fair to suggest that I detect some excuse making in your criticism? The burden to carry on the witness is now on you, and it is a relief to change the subject to us.

We are all in the same danger that surrounded Peter. Satan desires to have all of us, "to sift us as wheat," as Jesus said to Peter. Part of the sifting is the same today as it was when Peter stood by the fire in the courtyard when Jesus was first accused. We don't want to suffer or to give up anything—the image we have of ourselves or the way we think people perceive us. In *that* direction we accept the statement that the servant will get the same as the master. To avoid it, we don't like to make a big thing of our discipleship.

We don't want to take up our crosses and follow him. We join in Peter's rebuke, "God forbid, Lord! This shall never happen to you" (Matt. 16:22). Part of it is the fervent wish that our Lord not have to suffer. Part of it is that we even more fervently wish that we could share the glory without sharing the cross. But part of it, too—I think I'm probably making excuses again—part of it is that it isn't easy to comprehend nor to explain how going through all that ignominy, being mocked and spit upon and finally dying that degrading death on the cross, does us any good—especially not when 12 legions of angels and a little fire from heaven could have straightened the whole mess out in a lot less time than the three hours of darkness. What was difficult to grasp was that all that happened was a terrible visual aid for us. It was teaching us that God was willing to bear the brunt of all our sinning, to suffer its punishment for us and so free us from death and its terror. How could ordinary people have ever guessed that God planned the offering of God's Son, and that by his death we would be made free, saved?

Perhaps our reluctance to accept all this was because it was a gift, something simply to accept, and accepting meant admitting both our guilt and our weaknesses. It is a hard thing to swallow—that we can do nothing. We didn't want to admit it; we didn't want to accept it. That was at the root of our slowness of heart to understand and believe and our slowness to be witnesses.

A chill covers me as I think this through, a chill like that evening in the courtyard, and I would welcome a fire of coals to warm me. The voices Peter heard were accusing, taunting, because he was a disciple. The voices we hear are often uninterested, or lonely, or desperate. We fail to hear how those voices are masking a longing for a salvation they do not know. But we hear the same cock crow that Peter heard.

Ask not for whom the rooster crows. It crows for you.

Enough of what we haven't done. Better, no doubt, to talk about what God has done. We want to receive power from on high to speak our word for Jesus Christ. To remember positively what God-in-Christ has done for us is to let the Word move us anew. Think for a minute about what we might have done if we *had* understood, if we *had* asked questions, if Jesus *had* thought we were competent to bear it all then. Think about how we would have acted had you been with us then, knowing all you know now of how Jesus was laying down his life to take it up again, knowing that he was the Lamb of God dying to take away the sins of the world, that they were not taking his life from him but he was laying it down of himself as a ransom for the sins of the world, and that on the third day he would rise again for our justification—the first fruits of all mortals—and that we too who live and believe in him will never die. Consider what then we might have done! It might help us comprehend how great a thing it is he did without our aid and comfort.

There they come, the mob with swords and staves. We draw back to one side, but we do not flee. Now we know the mystery of salvation. The drama of atonement is beginning. We are a kind of Greek chorus of shadowed figures watching Jesus at center stage, watching in awe as the drama begins, no sword drawn, knowing that God is not sparing his only begotten Son but delivering him up for us all. They bind Jesus and lead him off to Annas and Caiaphas, and we follow, not a great way off, but not getting in God's way either.

The disciple who was well-known to the High Priest gets us all into the courtyard, and we stand with Peter, warming ourselves at the fire of coals. "You are also disciples of that man," the servant girl says, and she means all of us. "Your speech betrays you."

How much, now, we want to put into words all that we love and believe about this Jesus, so that our speech would really reveal our discipleship. Would one of us say quietly, "Not only our dialect. Let us tell you about him in so many words." And then we would say, taking turns, some of the obvious things first:

"He is no criminal. He is the best of all men."

"No one ever taught as he taught."

"Even the winds and the sea obey him."

"He made the blind to see and the lame to walk."

"This is the one who brought Lazarus back alive from the grave."

Then we would be bold enough to deepen our witness:

"We believe and are sure that this is the Messiah, the Son of the living God."

"Now you see no beauty in him that you should desire him, but he is being stricken, smitten of *God* and afflicted. He is being wounded for all our transgressions and bruised for all our iniquities. The chastisement of our peace is upon him and by his stripes we are all being healed."

All of us are standing there in a semicircle, an occasional flicker of flame from the coals lighting up our faces. Jesus turns to look into the courtyard at Peter, expecting to hear the cock crow. He sees us all there, and we see him. Each of us, each in a different way, urges him on, gesturing with our hands and fists, "Go, Jesus! Go!" Jesus turns back to the blindfolding and the mocking. Peter weeps, and we all weep, but there is a momentary and half smile on the face of the Savior.

And no cock crows.

When all that evil can do, evil has done, they put the cross, rough, on his scourged shoulder. We slip out and follow Simon the Cyrenean to a street corner where he knows the procession will pass. The soldiers and the mob are coming up the roadway, the roaring and the mocking noise increasing. Suddenly the soldiers grab Simon and compel him to carry the cross which has weighed Jesus to his knees on the street. As the procession pauses, we infiltrate the crowd around him. As the soldiers watch, dumbfounded (they say nothing, they do nothing, they can't imagine it happening), every hundred yards or so (we have the schedule of turns worked out) another one of us takes over the cross and follows him. My turn, his turn, your turn. And so up the hill of a skull, to Golgotha.

Without planning, without really talking about it, we take places in a ragged circle around the crosses, not to hold off the soldiers, not to block the plan that was in the mind of God before the foundation of the world, but to be there, to be there for him, with him. We know that here our dying is being done by him who knew no sin but now is made sin by God, who is forsaking him. We are close enough that when he is able to turn his head and look about, he can see us all, as well as Mary, his mother, and John, and the other women, and Jairus's daughter, perhaps, with the other teenagers, all of us with them in this circle of the church, determined to know nothing now but Jesus Christ and him crucified. All of you are there, in that circle, all of you knowing with anguish and yet with joy that everything is accomplished, all is forgiven, even as we hear his sturdy cry of "It is finished!" All of us join in one great human sigh, "Amen!" And many of us, for the first time, devoutly make the sign of the cross.

Ask not for whom the Savior dies. He dies for you.

Then, not many can help, but all those that Joseph and Nicodemus and their helpers need move up to the cross and gently follow the quiet instructions.

"Take the nails."

"Lift gently."

"Take his body now, his blood. Here, this napkin."

WHAT HAPPENED NEXT?

"Now, together, to my tomb in the garden. Its first and great guest."

Many hands make light work of the great stone. When it is in place, we all go to ours. There still is fear, yes, but we know now. We understand. The anxiety is more from counting the hours so that we will all be ready as the third day dawns.

Early in the morning the first day of the week as the sun begins to dawn, see us all standing there, one by one and in small groups, a straggling corridor along the path that leads from the sepulcher, faces all turned toward the mystery of faith, there, the sepulcher. "Christ has died! Christ is risen! Christ will come again!"

The earthquake, the angel in bright white, like lightning his appearance. All our eyes are blinded too, so that we all will know the blessedness of those who have not seen and yet have believed. Then we see the stone *is* rolled away; the place where he lay, empty. The firstborn from the dead, the only begotten Son of God, the Risen One, walks between the rows of us, straightened up to form a corridor. He stands for a moment like the gardener to speak to Mary Magdalene where the lilies grow.

And what do we do, all of us, standing there while the Savior, King of kings and Lord of lords, yet so clearly our brother still, goes by? Have we all been thinking, wondering, what to do, how to greet or speak or wave, standing here this last hour, knowing it is not something one can clap for, not a time for applause, nor for cheers even through our tears? Time for these, yes, but through them, smiles of thanksgiving and victory, time for pure adoration that this, God's Son, who was dead is alive, and we who were lost are found. The best I have been able to decide for myself, amid all those other things, is gently to pound my right hand formed in a fist into my half-closed left, saying over and over as I watch his coming, "Power! Power! Power and riches and wisdom and strength and honor and glory and praise be

He Goes with You

unto our God and to the Lamb forever and ever!" Then as the First and the Last, the Living One, goes past, my eyes and my smile and my joy, but my hands folded palm to palm, right thumb over left, "Kyrie! Lord and Christ!"

Ask not for whom the Savior rose. He rose for you.

Then we all seem to fall into line, following as the Lord leads—Is it 40 days?—up to the mount, he in the midst of us, speaking of the *paraclete* and power from on high. Knowing what we know, and realizing he is soon to be lifted from our sight to be with us all always, everywhere, centuries through, knowing all this, would there not be one of us— maybe Dorcas or Mrs. Zebedee, or the widow or Anne or Thaddaeus or the man who came through the roof or the three from the vineyard or the two from Emmaus or Mercy or Tom or Dick or—wouldn't it be great!—you or I who would be aware enough this time around, before the ascension, to go up to the Lord in the pause before he raises his arms in a benediction, and take his hand and say once out loud, before he is taken out of our sight, for all of us, say, "Thanks! Thank you, Lord Jesus, a lot!"

Then, while we behold, we hear, "All authority in heaven and on earth has been given to me. Go therefore and make disciples ... and lo, I am with you always, to the close of the age" (Matt. 28:18,20).

Ask not with whom the Savior goes. He goes with you.

❦

> O Master, let me walk with you
> In lowly paths of service true;
> Tell me your secret; help me bear
> The strain of toil, the fret of care.
>
> Help me the slow of heart to move
> By some clear, winning word of love;
> Teach me the wayward feet to stay,
> And guide them in the homeward way.

WHAT HAPPENED NEXT?

Teach me your patience; share with me
A closer, dearer company,
In work that keeps faith sweet and strong,
In trust that triumphs over wrong,

In hope that sends a shining ray
Far down the future's broad'ning way,
In peace that only you can give;
With you, O Master, let me live.

Lutheran Book of Worship, 492

Lenten Resources

The following Lenten resources are available from Augsburg Publishing House:

Where Is God in My Suffering? by Daniel J. Simundson

Simundson uses biblical texts about suffering and the suffering of Jesus to respond to questions Christians face today. A fine book for use during the Lenten season, it also is a biblical book of comfort for all those who suffer.

Preaching the Theology of the Cross by Peter L. Steinke

This probing book interprets Luther's theology of the cross and proclaims the God who shows wisdom in foolishness and strength in weakness. Steinke uses nine passages from the Bible to show how the cross of Christ puts all things to the test.

WHAT HAPPENED NEXT?

Upper Room to Garden Tomb by Herbert E. Hohenstein

Hohenstein shares eight fresh and insightful sermon resources for use in Lenten worship. The sermons focus on the Passion narrative according to St. Mark and are arranged chronologically. Lessons from Jesus' responses to those stressful events are applied to our lives. Included are sermons for the weeks in Lent, Good Friday, and Easter Sunday.

Gospel Dramas by Dean Nadasdy

This book contains two series of easy-to-perform dramas based on Lenten texts. The 12 plays offer ways to enliven worship in Lent and other seasons. Each drama is followed by "primers for preaching" on the play's theme and discussion questions for use with groups.

Sounds of the Passion by David M. Owen

In eight meditations Owen relates the sounds heard on the journey to Calvary to Jesus' life and death and to our own lives. These meditations can be a rich source of sermon ideas and also are excellent reading for individuals during the Lenten season.